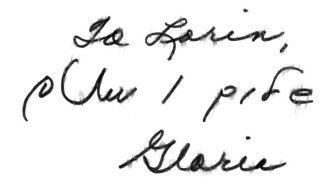

Shalom in My Heart,

Salaam on My Lips

A Jewish Woman in Modern Morocco

D1606402

Gloria Becker Marchick

Shalom In My Heart, Salaam On My Lips: A Jewish
Woman In Modern Morocco, Copyright © Gloria
Becker Marchick, 2003.

Except for the author's family, all names in this
book are fictitious.

Cover by Robert Hallman
Printed in the U.S.A.
0-916288-48-X

Micah Publications, Inc.
www.micahbooks.com

"You will go to the land of Allah."

"And what will I see there?"

"You must tell me."

To Ali

PREFACE

This book would not have been possible without the encouragement of my family who lived every minute of this adventure with me. The greatest hero was my husband Dick Marchick who spent three months with me in Tanger. He was a real trooper.

In addition, Chuck Nesbitt, Cindy Black Silver, Ona Jean Kraft Scott, and Elena Kutner e-mailed me every single day of my stay in Morocco. They were loyal beyond my wildest dreams. Everyday when I opened my e-mail, their names were brightly highlighted, waiting and caring for me. Billy Becker, Ruth Finkelstein, Chris Hawthorne, Zelda Schluker, Ruth B. Hurwitz, Tobey Olken, Ed Epstein, Elaine Marcus Starkman, Cindy Black Silver, Sally-Ann Fain Epstein, Rachel H. Kogan, Judy B. David, Howard Sidorsky, Susan Kemppainen, Patti M. Kogan, Noson Yanofsky, Emily Epstein, Barbara Budnitz, Adrian Blumberg, and Linda Morris slogged their way through unedited journal entries and manuscripts and encouraged me to share my adventure. Robert Hallman was the illustrious illustrator, cartographer, photographer, and cover designer extraordinaire. Without their support, these memories would have disappeared. I will be forever grateful for the opportunity I have had to share these uniquely private moments with a sympathetic audience.

i

I would also like to thank all the people in Morocco who accepted me, loved me, and tolerated and excused my *faux pas*. I never would have seen this private world without the hospitality of my Moroccan friends. My journey was terrifying at times, but a privilege and a revelation. I am grateful to have been part of events that are far greater than anything I had dreamed of. My only prayer is that this chapter in history will end in peace.

My story is just my story. It is also the story of some Moroccans. However, all of the Moroccan names are fictitious. All of the incidents are true.

PROLOGUE

I am a sixty-two-year old ordinary married woman with children and grandchildren. I teach English as a Second Language (ESL) at a local public adult school and also instruct teachers who are learning to teach ESL at the University of California. In 1995 I won a Fulbright TEFL (Teaching English as a Foreign Language) fellowship to teach at a university in Slovakia.

About two years ago, I decided to try for another Fulbright. I had already done the Eastern European tour and now I wanted to go to an exotic locale. So what did I consider exotic? I thought a non-European country would be challenging and interesting. I knew people who had visited Morocco and loved it, but I didn't know anyone who had lived there.

I began reading books about Morocco: *Sheltering Sky* by Paul Bowles, *Culture Shock, Morocco, A Street in Marrakech*, and others. The more I read, the more enthusiastic I became and called people who knew people who knew people who had lived there and, finally, I determined that Morocco was for me.

The Fulbright process is a long and complicated one, so I sent in my application and waited for the results. I can still see myself jumping up and down at the mailbox where I opened the letter, in the cold, holding a stack of less important mail. What a wonderful feeling!

The Fulbright office in Washington D.C. was very helpful and again I began calling people, including a former Ambassador to Morocco, to ask how they liked living and working in Morocco. Everyone was encouraging. I e-mailed and called former Fulbright scholars whom I asked what five things they wished they had taken to Morocco that they hadn't taken. All of them commented on the cold winters. I had thought that the heat would be a problem but instead everyone talked about the cold. I knew that I would be prepared because I packed warm sweaters, long underwear and tights. I was ready.

A few people asked how I, a Jew, could go to an Arab country. My answer was simple. During World War II, King Mohammed V of Morocco refused to hand over his Jews to Hitler. When commanded to deliver the Jews, he replied to Hitler and the Vichy government, "I have no Jews. There are only Moroccan citizens living here." The 200,000 Moroccan Jews were saved. It is the one Arab country where there is still a viable Jewish community that lives, works, and worships freely.

The first three weeks I lived in Fes (Fez) where I attended an Arabic language school. I celebrated the Jewish holy days openly and with zealous joy. However, when I left and moved to teach at Abdelmalek Saadi University in Tetouan/Martil, the Al Aqsa Intifada broke out in late September, right after Rosh Hashanah. This uprising, or small undeclared war, in the Middle East between the Israelis and the Palestinians was usually reported by showing suicide bombers, burning tires, rock throwing and shooting; but this was a sanitized version that I witnessed on American television. The Arabic version showed more gore, maiming, and close-ups of death.

Intifada in an Arabic country was a different story than witnessed from the West. It was an integral component in the everyday life of each Moroccan citizen. Morocco went from being a depressed, Third World country without a purpose to being a shouting participant fueled by a war one thousand miles away—and all of the protest was against Israel and the Jews. With the outbreak of the Intifada, my experience as a Jew in an Arab land became radically different than I had ever imagined it would be. I soon realized that not only were Americans unpopular, but it was dangerous to be openly

iv

Jewish. I made the decision to remain in Morocco with one modification of behavior; I would not claim to be Jewish. When asked my religion, I responded, "*Je suis croyante,*" (I am a believer) which seemed to satisfy the questioners. I felt that an atheist would be viewed as someone to convert or avoid, whereas a believer could be anything. I hoped not to have to identify myself explicitly as something else and was able to avoid doing that. I assume that people thought I was a Christian, but I never asked.

If I had had the prescience to know there would be an Intifada maybe I would have changed my plans and would not have gone. After the Intifada began, the State Department issued warnings, the Israeli Embassy closed permanently, and the American Embassy had intermittent closures. There were protest marches where Israeli and American flags were burned. I got scared and felt that if something happened to a lone woman like me, who would know? Many days, and sometimes weeks, I was unable to reach my California home via the cell phone. The Internet was also out of order for days at a time. How long would it take for my family to start worrying about where I was? They were already worried about my safety but they assumed that every night I reached home. In hindsight, I think I had legitimate reasons to be afraid. What still confuses me is what drove me to stay.

My exploits in Morocco were both extraordinary and ridiculous. I pride myself on having a keen sense of humor which certainly saved me many times. However, in the end, it was the wonderful friends I made and the love with which I was treated that is the memory I cherish. I always felt deceitful because I refused to discuss my religion honestly with my beloved friends. I don't know what the experience would have been otherwise but I was too fragile and needy to take a chance on being abandoned. Even though I feel I may not have done justice to these incredible people, I am sorry that I could not be honest with them because fear prevented me from being otherwise. Hopefully, there will be another chance to resolve this lost opportunity.

I never realized how strong my Jewishness was and how it filtered the way I viewed my world. I had heard that the traveler learns most about herself, and my experience verified that. I not only learned about Morocco, but I learned who I am. Perhaps that is the reason for such a sojourn. I could not have lived in Morocco without changing and while I appear to be the same person today, I know that I will never be the same. For that, I am thankful. My daily journal entries reflect the changes, which are my treasured souvenirs from this extraordinary visit to Morocco.

This is what it was.

THE BEGINNING

September 1, 2000

Mohammed Jamel was my faculty sponsor. I met him when I got off the airplane September first. His instructions were to look for the lady with the red sandals.

When I exited customs, a tall tan man approached me and said, "You're the only one with red shoes, so you must be Gloria." I laughed and he sort of smiled. He drove me immediately to the four-star Reyes Hotel and left me because, he said, "You should rest. I'll pick you up at ten tomorrow so you can get anything you need."

"Thanks. *Merci. Shokrun*," I replied and went to my non-air-conditioned hotel room, looked at my suitcases, and started writing in my journal. I watched Arab TV, and unpacked and repacked my carry-on. I took long walks even though the thermometer registered over one hundred degrees. I walked around the hotel only to learn that no one spoke English. No one spoke French either. The gift shop was a counter opposite the reception desk so I counted the number of items for sale (fifty-six) and then tried to count them in French. I walked to the restaurant, which was closed. I looked at the bar, also closed. I sat in the lobby and began the whole ritual again. Sometimes I found that I counted fifty-eight items in the gift case. I was paralyzed. I had culture shock.

Jamel picked me up the next four mornings at ten o'clock and returned me to the hotel at one or two. He helped me buy a cell phone and look for apartments both in the adjacent communities of Tetouan/Martil and Tanger. He found my piece of lost luggage. He had a big smile, deep green eyes and tan ankles that always showed because he wore no socks. Yet he gave me nothing of himself and asked me nothing about myself.

I asked about his family and his education.

"I got my Ph.D. in England."

"How many years were you there?"

"I was there five years, but only one year was I alone. My wife came for the last four and Drissa was born there."

"No wonder you speak such beautiful English."

"I'm very westernized," he bragged.

I understood his perfectly articulated English but I had no idea about what was behind the words; what he said, what he thought and what he really meant. He was distant, controlled, authoritarian, and disinterested. His impervium was never penetrated.

I had decided to rent an apartment in Tanger because I loved the bustle of the city, so Jamel said he would pick me up the next day to sign the lease. However, when he arrived at ten, he said, "My wife and her friends decided you should rent the home we saw in Martil so you will be close to the university. Here you will really get to know the faculty."

We had looked at numerous apartments and one lovely house in Martil. But Martil appeared dead and devoid of activity. Other than beach activity, it was desolate. I had to admit its proximity to the university was a plus but I was scheduled to teach only two days a week.

I was uncomfortable but said, "I don't want to live in Martil."

He smiled and looked at me with those big green eyes magnified in nonreflective glass and said, "Trust me. This is the right decision." Without further explanation, he drove to Martil intent on getting rid of his charge. He was silent.

"Shouldn't you call the people first?"

"No, they're always home."

"I really don't want to live there"

"You shouldn't separate yourself from the faculty."

"My soul will be unhappy in that house," I said, unsure where this sentence had come from. It was a voice I had never heard before. It was met with silence.

I rented the house and stipulated it would be for one month only because I thought Tanger would be better for me. I couldn't figure out how I had allowed this to happen. Jamel sat in a straight back chair with a big grin on his face.

He helped me move into the home when he carried half the boxes and suitcases to the front door. My husband, Dick, later said that he felt Jamel probably got a kickback from the owner because he arranged this deal over the phone, which is why he did not need to call after he spoke to me the morning we signed the lease and why the owners were at home, waiting. I had probably been "sold" for a ten-dollar finder's fee.

The house in Martil was located in a summer vacation town that had been boarded up for the winter. I was the only inhabitant of my dismal block and every house I passed had locked shutters, locked gates and no signs of life. I was isolated. I was terrified. I was sad. And I was abandoned.

I saw Jamel twice after that. One time at the front gate of the university, I went up to him and said, "*Salaam* Jamel."

"How are you Gloria?"

"Fine. I'd like a minute of your time."

He stopped and leaned his six-foot frame towards me.

"Jamel, if I'd been any other kind of person and hadn't been strong, I would've perished in that house in Martil. Where were you?"

He paused for a second. "I didn't visit because I wanted you to meet the people...to get the feel of the country...not be dependent on me." Again, I watched those dark green eyes, full of contempt, look right at me as he spoke. He never blinked.

I walked away from him without even an acknowledgement of his reply because the words had no meaning. I felt as if I had no value and was just an object that needed to be placed somewhere, out of his way. I accommodated him. I stayed out of his way.

But there is a God, and he brought me Ismael Benbouhia. He is a social linguistics professor at Abdel Malik Saadi University who studied in England for about ten years where he got his Master's degree and his Ph.D. He then returned to Morocco with a Scottish wife, Elizabeth.

It is hard to describe Ismael. He is about five feet eight, ivory skinned, green eyes, very curly brown hair and full lips that display straight white teeth with one very dead black tooth. He reminds me of a teddy bear because he is neither angular nor hard looking. He is warm, funny, bright and charming. He is a master at self-deprecation and yet he can be quite erudite. His spoken English can be slang or lyrical. He is totally irreverent, brutally honest, and mischievous. He saved me from many *faux pas* and guided me every step of my journey through Morocco.

After just one day in the house in Martil, I told Ismael that I was about to sign a lease on the original flat I had seen with Jamel in Tanger. I would walk away from the Martil house and for one month would pay rent in both places. He told me that his brother, Adnane, had a rental unit in Tanger. I sort of hedged and said, "Thanks but I found a place."

"Why don't you just take a quick look at this flat? I lived there for four years. It's nice. Trust me. I know what foreigners like."

"Thanks, Ismael. I love this new place because it has a partial view of the sea. Besides, today I have an appointment to sign the lease."

"Gloria, it'll take ten minutes. At least you can say you were open to it."

"Okay Ismael, but will you take me to the train station after I look because I don't have any time. I need to get to the Arabic Language School in Fes."

So I looked. I stared. I gaped. I walked around the huge apartment. It was the most beautiful place I had ever been in and it was less money than the smaller one with a partial view. "Fantastic! *Pas mal!*" I shouted. "This is for me."

Ismael knew what was best. This apartment was one half block from the beach with nothing in front of it but an old one-story factory that was invisible from the seventh floor aerie. The floors were marble and in one of the front salons there were Greek pillars and a domed recess for the light fixture. The whole north side of the flat was glass. I felt I was perched on the shores of Spain. The flat had four bedrooms, two baths with toilets you could sit on and not just stoop over, two salons, a huge European dining room, a porch and a large modern kitchen. It would be luxurious in any country. "Fantastic! *Pas mal !*" I exclaimed.

A LIFE IN FES

September 5, 2000
(The anniversary of my mother's death and my grandson, Jacob's birthday.)
After the bittersweet days of the apartment search, my time with Jamel, and then the challenge to survive constant above one hundred degree days in Martil, I am happy to leave for the Arabic Language School in Fes where I am to stay for three weeks. I am frightened because of the new environment but I know that it cannot be worse than Martil. Hopefully, I will not be much older than the other students. I repeat the mantra I used to give my children when they were young; "All you need in the world is one friend."

The next twelve hours are tedious but the tedium is a relief from depression, tension and fear of Martil. The rhythm of the train is a welcome song plus the comfort of the first class cabin, thanks to the French Protectorate, is a luxury well deserved. Even though I had read the five books I carried in my luggage, I reread the *Poisonwood Bible* and think that I am in a wonderful place. For the first time in days, my appetite is enormous and seems to be an unwelcome friend who has returned to stay. So I am lucky they sell food on the train since I had eaten everything I had packed within minutes of the departure. It feels good to have a full stomach and not a knot in the gut.

I enroll at the Arabic Language Institute, get a single room at the dorm and decide to walk around Fes. The section that the school is in is part of the "New City," the area that was inhabited and built by the French. This quiet neighborhood has large villas surrounded by high, stuccoed walls that are at least ten feet tall. There are some apartment houses, two churches, a hospital plus the Zalagh Hotel in just a five-block area that has streets that are lined with a canopy of old olive trees. I walk for hours. At three o'clock I realize that I am lost, hungry, and overheated. I spend the next hour on the lookout for familiar landmarks but cannot find any.

I try not to panic and finally find a taxi sitting next to a curb. The driver doesn't look too friendly but I say in my very best French, *"Monsieur, s'il vous plaît, je voudrais aller a l'hotel Zalagh."* (I would like to go to the Zalagh Hotel, please.) The school is located diagonally across from the Zalagh and the dormitory is next door so I know that I will be all right once I get to the hotel. However, the taxi driver does not move even though I am sure he has heard me. Again, I repeat my request in polite French and he mumbles something in Arabic. I tell him I am sorry but I would really like to go to the Zalagh, *"maintenant!"* The "now" seems to stir him up so he starts the taxi and yells at me in Arabic. I feel quite powerful since I am able to incur such wrath with what I consider a simple French request. He guns the engine, shifts into first gear which he maintains the entire forty seconds it takes to drive me from the back entrance to the front entrance of the Zalagh Hotel.

"Oye!" I say to myself. "Now what are you going to do?" The first thing I do is pay double what the meter displays, exit the taxi, and limp dramatically towards my blessed dormitory room in the villa. I fight to stifle a laugh, especially since there is no one around with whom I can share the first of many infamous taxi rides.

The dormitory and its students are my world for three weeks in Fes. Here international students are united in an effort to learn Arabic. The teachers are excellent and the students are outstanding. Both Classical Arabic and Moroccan Arabic are taught daily to scholars and to hopeless language learners like me. Classical Arabic is used in all written Arabic language documents from newspapers to the Koran, whereas, each Arabic country has its own dialect and, in fact, each city in Morocco has a slightly different dialect. The common language of the Arab world is Classical Arabic, which only the educated can speak while ordinary Arabs are unable to understand the other dialects unless the countries are geographically close. On a tour of the Hassan II Mosque, I met a Syrian family who took the English tour because the woman said, "We cannot understand the language these people speak."

"Isn't it all Arabic?" I asked.

"No, spoken Arabic reflects the country where it is spoken." I assumed she meant that each country has a unique dialect. However, she was not the last to explain the problem to me.

The students at the dormitory live in a three-story walled villa that has a grand winding marble staircase that is at least ten feet wide. The floors are white marble, as are part of the walls in many of the first floor rooms. During the summer period all the students have their own rooms but we share a common bath. Michal, Hans, Liesl and Astrid are German students who are majors in some area of Islamic studies. Hamid is a Sri Lankan boy from UCLA who wants to understand Arabic when he prays as a devout Moslem. Jeremy is a blonde kid from Chicago who speaks five languages and wants to learn a sixth. Erik is a single Norwegian man in his forties who represents a mobile-phone company in the North African Arab world. Bianca and Nora do not live in the Villa because they say they are a bit older than the other students are. Bianca is in Morocco on a student Fulbright and Nora is a state department employee who has just finished a three-year stint at the American Embassy in Jordan. Renat is an Israeli woman in her thirties who is working on a Master's degree in comparative religions at Ben Gurion University and is fluent in Palestinian Arabic. I am a sixty-two year old woman who is about to begin a year-long teaching fellowship as a Fulbright professor in Northern Morocco.

That night I hook up with Michal, from Germany and Nora, the African American woman from Tennessee, who has put herself through undergraduate and graduate school. She beams when she declares, "I'm the first one in my family to graduate high school."

The three of us go to dinner at a touristy Moroccan restaurant and sit for three hours enjoying each other's company.

Nora tells us, "I loved working in Jordan. I'm really going to miss my friends. They taught me all the bad Arabic words I know," she laughs. "The government is picking up the check for my three months here so I can improve my Arabic."

"Are you living in the dorm?" I ask.

"No. I wanted some privacy," she answers. Yet Nora spends every evening in the dorm with all of us because she loves the camaraderie that developed here. Suddenly, she starts to talk about the Israeli-Arab conflict.

"Our government sucks because they give so much money to Israel," she says.

"I thought that the Jordanian budget depended on American funds also, Nora."

"Well, it does but Israel has all that Jewish help."

"I have Arab friends in the U.S. whose women's group sends tens of thousands of dollars to the Middle East and they are probably the smallest donors to the Arab world." I mention this without letting her know I am Jewish.

"Well, the Israelis are so tough on the Jordanians who go to see their relatives in Israel. My friends hate to go through customs."

"Nora, how will they ever stop the arms smugglers if they don't check the visitors?"

"My friends don't carry guns," she says defiantly. "The Jordanians are victims of Israeli oppression."

Finally, I ask, "Nora, I never understood Jordanian policy. Can you help me? I've always wondered why, with Jordan so outspoken about the creation of a Palestinian State, why didn't they create the state of Palestine during the twenty years they held the disputed land?"

She sits silently and finally says, "They should've but no one talks about that."

I decide not to continue.

"I always went to Israel for my weekends off because it's so liberal there and I never had a bad time. Besides, the Israeli dudes are studs."

Michal has been silently frozen there as he drinks his wine. Finally, Nora turns to him and says, "Michal, why do you Germans give so much money to Israel?"

At first, Michal remains silent. His chiseled face is stone. I am not sure what his thoughts are. I look at his shaved head and am reminded of the Jews in the camps. Finally, he looks up. I think I see his eyes cloud up but I am sure it is my imagination.

"Nora, we are ashamed. We have no excuse for what we did. The money is nothing. I could never forgive my grandfather for being a Nazi. He came back from the war different and never recovered. I think that is really like Germany. We can never recover from what we did. The money is nothing."

We sit quietly for a few minutes. Each of us mulls over the conversation. I think about my Jewishness and the advantage of its secrecy. I am learning too much by being "nothing." We finish dinner and walk back to the "New City."

The next day more students arrive and while they are young, they are older than eighteen. There is a large contingent from Germany, a couple of Americans, three Swiss women and a Norwegian. Everyone is friendly which creates a harmonious atmosphere in the villa. We quickly become a family and learn about each other in our other lives. No one leaves the villa without a poll to see if anyone wants to join him or her or if anyone needs anything at the store. It is a wonderful place to be. Here, I smile a lot and often.

Our favorite place in Fes is the Medina, the old city. Everyday after class, groups of students go to the Medina just as American teenagers love to go to a mall. It is our hangout. We eat food from the stands, bargain for souvenirs, go to the community baths, and then return to do the same thing after dinner. It is never the same group that shares a taxi or a bus, but it is invariably a group.

The Medina is always an adventure. It is at least 1000 years old, a maze of narrow streets where businesses and living quarters are crowded with thousands of people, sounds, smells and sights. This hot night, there are crowds that stroll through the streets and seem to have no destination. The men and women jostle us without a word of apology. Half of the people wear long robes called *jallabahs*. I assume they wear something underneath. Many of the robed women also wear headscarves or *hajabs*, and some wear veils, which cover two thirds of their faces. The noise of the voices is deafening and there are always children who play and yell in the middle of the eight-foot-wide cobblestone streets. Donkeys, the delivery truck of the Medina, make their way through the multitude of people, while those resourceful souls who have no donkey, push brakeless carts with huge wheels that help them deliver their goods. They yell *"Balak!"* ("Watch Out!") and when we hear it, we jump quickly to either side of the street so the ever-present animals will not run into us nor will the unstoppable carts run over us.

The smells of the Medina change at every cross street. The spice streets are pungent with the aroma of curry, garlic and cinnamon that permeate the walkway. The worst section is the odorous fish and meat section. Huge chunks of beef and lamb dangle from hooks while blood drips into the streets. At the end of the day, dried blood is caked on the counters and cobblestones in the meat section. This produces a wafting putrid smell that nauseates me. My nostrils can never be cleansed of the stench that has settled in my every pore. The odor is indescribable and it causes me to gag. The butchers also display the once peaceful, now grotesque, dazed heads of animals, lined up on the counter ostensibly to watch the parade of shoppers. It is impossible for a passerby to miss them and, for a vegetarian like me, this is wretched. The fish section is worse. I breathe through my mouth and pant like Lamaze mothers-to-be so that I can stifle my gag reflex. There is also the stench of dung from the ubiquitous donkeys. In this medley of smells and high humidity, dung is stronger than all the other odors.

In spite of the sensory stimuli, we laugh, kid each other, and have a wonderful walk. Each of us has our favorite section or stall that we visit regularly. Stall keepers get to know us and give us samples of dates, nuts, and fruits. We cannot get enough on our trays and we hate to leave.

On this night, Astrid and Liesl, my German friends, Saadia, the maid from the dorm, and I spend our evening in the Medina. It is cooler now, but it is still in the high 80s. The buzz deafens and the frantic energy invigorates us.

Whether there are fixed price signs or not, it is a badge of honor to bargain. I feel like a failure if I pay the full price for anything. I try on about fifteen pairs of pointed slippers and finally find one that sort of fits. We learn to bargain when Saadia shows us how to negotiate like a professional as she haggles for slippers for everyone and tea glasses for me. She is young and beautiful with straight black hair, exquisite black eyes, full lips, and absolutely perfect teeth. She is immaculately dressed and quite thin. She is also illiterate, single and poor. I got a glimpse of her bedroom the other day when I went up to the roof to hang my laundry on the clothesline. The room is in the center of the roof and is only slightly wider than her single bed. There is one glassless window in her room which, has an ill-fitting screen on it. I assume she boards it up during the cold winter. There is no electricity and the door does not close well. She speaks no English but makes motions like an airplane and says, "Gloria, Saadia, America." I kiss her cheeks to seal the make-believe contract. We both know that she will never get to America and probably has no hope of any better life than that of the maid at the villa – which is actually a sought after position because she gets a free room. She is very devout and I find her on her knees on her prayer rug at all times of the day. I feel like the constant intruder who contaminates her holy space.

We take her out to dinner to a lovely restaurant near the school. She won't order, so I take out my wallet, point to my money and say "Saadia, Gloria, *minfadlik,*" which means "please" in Arabic. She finally orders some kind of kabob. We have no idea if she has ever been to a restaurant. She watches our actions closely and does not take a bite until we do. It is a wonderful evening with laughs, an exchange of grunts, and one-word sentences.

I wake up the next morning refreshed but still sort of sweaty, however, now I expect that to be the norm in Fes. Class is difficult. I find that I get so tense that I block out the Arabic and think of anything but what I should think of. Benki, the instructor, will not turn on the overhead fan in this third floor classroom because he tells us that last year one of the fans fell on a teacher and cut him badly. Now he takes no chances. I watch his shirt get wetter and wetter. A mole shows through the fabric on the front of his left shoulder. My legs are wide apart because I hope the 100-degree air will circulate under my skirt. My arm sticks to my notebook. My attention span is nonexistent. Someone in the class has BO and I wonder if I do not smell myself.

Erik sits across from me. We make a pitiful attempt to isolate the sound of the Arabic letter O. Finally, Erik yells, "I've got it!" He lifts his sandaled foot and points to his big toe and says "O as in toe." Benki huffs and the class starts to laugh and can't stop. The hysterics break the tension we feel because of the difficulty of Arabic combined with the oppressive heat and the seriousness of our instructor. We probe Benki for life but find none. He never stops his spiel nor does he respond to questions other than with, "It will become quite clear in the next section." We roll our eyes and look away from him. The tension continues to mount and Benki gets even more determined to finish his monologue. However, we cannot listen and start to laugh again. Benki explodes and tells us he has never had such terrible students. We look at our books because if we raise our eyes, we laugh harder. Benki continues to produce isolated guttural sounds while we sit like medicated lunatics.

Thanks to Allah, class is over. I need to buy AA batteries. I am not very creative so on a white 3 X 5 card I draw a picture of two horizontal cylinders with a black circle in the center of a larger circle on one end of the cylinder. I go to a radio store, telephone store, bookstore, grocery store and tobacco store. At each establishment, when I show my illustrated card, the clerk shakes his head no and shrugs. Finally, I go to my new e-mail provider where I show the card to him and also to one of the hundreds of boys, who are not in school but who just hang around. Mohammed replies in Arabic, "*Nam*," which means "yes" and yes, he will definitely get four (*arba*) for me. I don't know why I did not think of the cyber café before to solve this quest. Smugly, I begin my e-mail correspondence for the day where I recount the success of my clever mind. Ten minutes later, a boy runs in with a huge smile on his face and he tosses four packs of Marlboros to me. I pay him and give the cigarettes to the cyber café attendant.

The inability to communicate frightens me. I am dumfounded and feel stupid and helpless. Luckily, there is a hotel nearby. I walk in and ask if anyone speaks English and I find a man with a fifty-word English vocabulary who tells me to go to a magazine kiosk and show the picture of the batteries to the man at the counter who should have some batteries. To him, it is logical that a magazine kiosk should have batteries. To me, it is illogical and I realize I still think like an American.

The kiosk at the end of the street does have batteries and I am the last sale before the owner closes the shutters to retire until three o'clock.

I pick up some cheese, tomatoes, yogurt, bread and the Bimo Tonik cookies that I purchase every day for ten cents from a street peddler. I return to the villa for lunch and to study. The cat comes in. I yell at him to leave because I am terribly allergic. When he won't leave, I throw a small plastic basket at him. He runs outside while I grin at my success. I love this lunch and lunchtime activity. What is even better, I grab a nap and miss the hottest part of the day. I am sure if the roof were removed from all the houses around here right now a bird would see rooms of one hundred-and-twenty degree filled with comatose people exactly like me. I am lucky that I can sleep in the oppressive heat.

There is some kind of horse celebration tonight, but no one knows exactly where it is. I go to a taxi stand with Astrid, Liesl, Hamid, and Erik where we take *petit* taxis, half the size of the usual Mercedes, to a huge field. Here, hundreds, if not thousands of people, form a rectangle around a dry, dusty racetrack. What this means is that there is a field of about a fifty-yard rectangle that has no rope or barrier while there are twenty-five horses with riders in white robes and headdresses who carry silver and wooden rifles. At the sound of a single gunshot, all the horses run as fast as their riders can get them to run, to the end of the field. There is no fence, no barricade, nothing to stop them, and they try to stop about ten feet in front of the line of people. Then the riders fire a round of shots into the air. It is marvelous in its disorganized organization. Erik thinks he read about this in his guidebook because he says it commemorates something but no one knows what.

"This is called Fantasia," he says. "I think these people come from the country and live on this field for a week but I am not sure." We laugh because it doesn't matter to us what it is. Just before the next starting shot, kids run across the field to see if they can beat the horses. Most of the time I close my eyes because I cannot witness how narrowly disaster misses. There is one policeman who patrols each side of the rectangle and he yells at the deaf crowd to stay back but the people in back can neither see nor hear him. They push all the sides closer. Hamid and I sneak through the line so we can stoop in front to see the action. When the horses come toward us, I scream and close my eyes while Hamid prays like crazy to Allah. One of these actions works because we do not get trampled. However, we are covered with a thin layer of dust that turns Hamid's coal black hair to salt and pepper gray and his glasses opaque. We both taste dust. We know we cannot stay where we are so we crawl through the legs of hundreds of people and walk around the tents where the riders live during this horse celebration week. I don't know what keeps away deaths and accidents since there is no thought to safety.

Erik rides back in the petit taxi with me. "Gloria, why do you always look so happy?"

"Erik dear, I may look happy, but each day and each hour is a challenge to survive."

"But Gloria, you make it look easy."

"Erik, I am a phony."

He touches my cheek with two soft fingers and smiles.

He buys me some sugared nuts from a street vendor. The nuts are weighed with a rock as the counter-weight. Then the vendor tears a page out of an old book and folds the paper into a cone that he fills with nuts. He uses his dirty hand to transfer them from the scale to the paper holder. I have washed my hands for one month with some kind of waterless bacteria fighter from America and now I watch a dirty hand place nuts into a dirty page from an old book.

I figure, "What the hell! I won't die from this." Erik and I consume one rock's worth of delicious sugared nuts.

We return to the villa where I eat cheese, bread and yogurt for dinner. Luckily, I was able to find a store with Coca-

Cola Light so I drink something that I love and that makes me feel like I am not so far away from home. I buy two bottles of Sidi Ali mineral water every morning but manage to lose both by noon. I always retrace my route and where I have stopped to sit down but the bottles are never there. I have to figure out how to keep everything together.

Astrid shares some delicious cookies with me. The cat comes in and, again, I yell at him to get out. He glares at me this time when I pick up the plastic clothesbasket and runs before I can throw it at him. I have taught the cat a trick!

I study Arabic for six hours tonight. I am about to cry because it is so difficult. I am not sure why I enrolled in Classical Arabic. I had originally signed up for Moroccan Arabic but Nora said, "Girl, if you go to any other Arab country, they won't know what you are talking about." I had plans to go to other Arab countries and especially to go to Ber Sheba, Israel, to teach teachers how to instruct the Bedouins in English. So Nora helped me switch to Classical Arabic.

However, Hamid looks at me with his ebony eyes and says, "Why are you taking Classical Arabic? The only reason for that is to study the Koran." Damn it. I don't want to read the Koran. The reality is that I want to be able to buy eggs and read nonexistent street signs. I realize that I have been in the wrong class. I am so upset that at two o'clock when I finally turn out my light, I cannot sleep. I do not know how to contain this anxiety and there is no one I can talk to. I return to my desk and practice the Arabic alphabet only to realize that there is some peace in the repetition of sounds and the calligraphy of each letter.

I walk out on the porch. Astrid's light is still on in her room. Even though she is years ahead of me in Arabic, I can hear her chant in chorus with the tapes. I spend another hour with my tapes and headphones in a futile effort to maintain the position as the worst student in the class.

At four in the morning I wake up with terrible cramps and run towards the bathroom. I don't make it. Just like a kid, I have the worst diarrhea and just short of my target is a shower of shit. I am covered with stool and struggle to hold back my tears. I strip naked and throw my nightgown and slippers into the sink. Then I jump into the shower. Someone has left a towel draped over two hooks. I dry myself with it and know that if I just rehang it, it will be bone dry in the morning. Hopefully, the owner will never know it dried my shitty body.

But now I have a problem with the floor. I wrap the towel around me and run downstairs where I find some rags in Saadia's bucket in the kitchen. I tote soap powder and bleach upstairs and go down on my hands and knees to clean up shit until five in the morning. As I wash the grout between the gray tiles of the bathroom, I suddenly stop and look at a 62-year-old woman on her knees on the floor. Here I am, buck naked, in a common bathroom.

I was so upset about the diarrhea, the stool on the floor, my nightie and myself that I never considered what would happen if someone walked in. I laugh as I think what a pitiful figure I have become. At 5:15, I hear Hamid get up to say his prayers. I jump up and carry my clothes, rags, bucket and slippers into my room where I slam the door shut.

I sit down on my cot and inhale deeply about ten times. I think I will be able to sleep now. Three hours later I wake up, still sitting on my bed, stark naked, with someone else's towel clutched in my hand and a bucket of rags on my lap. I am too exhausted to even care. I lie down and go back to sleep. I cannot tell whether this is the end of one day or the beginning of another.

WILLIE AND FRED

The first personal survival commandment I had that I broke during my stay in Morocco was not to seek fellow Americans. But there was one time that I went out of my way to do it. As an instructor who lectures on how to succeed during prolonged stays in foreign lands, my basic tenets begin with "Don't associate with the expatriate subculture. You will create a mini-America in a foreign land." I believe this is true and can cite examples of people who never meet a native in their new milieu. However, Willie and Fred were dear friends of Lew, my husband's Harvard buddy.

Willie and Fred have been together forty years. They are the owners of the Gay Erotic Art Museum in Manhattan and they also manage their own foundation that funds gay and lesbian artists. They are well respected, brilliant, charitable and hilarious. They have a home in Marrakech that they visit twice a year. Luckily, one of their visits coincided with my stay.

I contacted Willie and said, "Here I am!"

"Come see our Marrakech."

"I'll be on the late train. You'll recognize me because I have red sandals and always look lost."

"We'll find you."

It was a very long train ride that was three hours late, yet at midnight on a Friday I was met at the train by a perfect stranger who said, "Welcome to Marrakech. *Bienvenue á Marrakech.*"

Willie had rust colored hair, robin egg blue eyes, straight, beautifully whitened teeth; a straw hat cocked slightly to the right and was strikingly handsome in varying shades of tan. His equally handsome Moroccan driver smiled and said, "*La bas.*"

"La bas," I echoed, shook his hand, and touched my heart.

We drove through Marrakech, the city whose palette consists of five shades of terracotta on the exterior walls of all the buildings. It is definitely the jewel of Morocco. Willie, who blended into the color spectrum of Marrakech, gave a well-organized historical and cultural tour. However, this tour was different as it revealed a part of Morocco that no one else had mentioned.

"There's a large gay population here."

"Are most of them Moroccan?"

"No, but the Moroccans are tolerant of us. It's cheap to live here for foreigners and they welcome our financial input. The economy here has been bad for a long time so with each of us who buys a house here, we employ full-time year-round domestics, which is important for their workforce."

We arrive at the Medina, which, unlike the one in Fes, allows some vehicular traffic on the narrow streets. There is a small parking lot guarded by three attendants.

"They are here twenty-four hours a day and two of them are college graduates. Hello Driss." He greets the nearest young man with a hug. His commentary continues, "Driss feels lucky to have this job since he is the only one in his whole family who works."

We walk about one block to a narrow alley. We wander down a lane that is no wider than nine feet and is surrounded by fifteen-foot walls. I stumble on the uneven steps and irregular stones in the dark passageway. However, after a few minutes, a magnificently polished wooden door greets us and when it opens, it is a veritable garden.

Willie said, "This is a typical old Moroccan home, my humble digs!"

"You have trees in your house!"

"And birds. Look out below!"

The center courtyard is the focal point of these traditional old homes. This dark brick colored house has two floors that surround the courtyard and every room overlooks the beautiful garden. They have refurbished it and modernized the bathrooms and kitchen, yet have ensured that the ancient grandeur is undisturbed. Intricate tile patterns form walkways through the garden, and then lead to different rooms on the first floor. The balconies and shuttered windows of the second floor overlook the garden and create an intimacy of a private mysterious world hidden from the noises of the outside world. There is a large tiled fountain that bubbles in the center of the courtyard.

The young man who accompanied us from the train station, Ibrahim, has to return to his home two hours away. Ibrahim, a fireman, is also gay, Willie informs me. "He feels he would be ostracized in his town if he publicly admits his homosexuality. But here, in the Medina, in this haven, with us, he's safe. At forty-five, he still lives with his parents and his excuse to them is that he cannot afford a wife yet, but when he saves enough money, he will get married." Ibrahim leaves us at one in the morning to return to his other life.

There are two other men on staff at this house. Both men are gay and one had been homeless when Willie somehow found him. "They live here full-time and maintain the house. They also keep it safe from vandals and burglars," he continues. His chatty, friendly conversation never stops

"Poverty is a constant companion to the general Moroccan population and when you have nothing, when you have no food, no house, no job, no hope and you find an empty house, as a 'have-not' you become creative in order to find a way to make your life better. You acquire from others. So there is a need for constant surveillance of the homes of the 'haves' because they are the targets of many burglaries."

There is a huge dog that lives in the house. He is a big, native mutt, larger than a German shepherd, who was near death in the street and he, like the houseboy, was saved by Willie.

"Our friends say that when they come back in their next life, they want to be either an employee or pet of ours. Both are treated like royalty."

Dogs are not pampered in Morocco and are almost as badly abused as the donkey, which is the most abused animal in the whole country. In fact, many Moroccans are afraid of dogs, perhaps because the dog is generally used to ward off strangers and is not cosseted like Western dogs. This flatulent dog was an ugly African dog that supposedly was descended from the original dog and was the only heterosexual male in the house. Unfortunately, I was the only female and it was with me that he wanted to be amorous. Whenever he was not held down, he would bounce off any part of me that he could make contact with. I told him that I hated dogs, was married, and was committed to having a Jewish home. Still, he lunged at me every time Willie let go of his collar, even though he had been commanded to sit. I was not flattered.

My ancient bed, with its exotic Arabic pillows, had a bedspread with large silver discs all over it that I had to remove because every time I turned over I caused a jingle. The shutters to my window were tightly closed but the birds' chorus began at 5:30 in the morning and woke me to a beautiful sunny day. I opened the shutters, looked up at the clear blue sky and down at the different rooms opening onto the center courtyard. Colorful Moroccan rugs covered the tiled floors and the walls were decorated with tapestries, paintings and ancient Arabic artifacts. I felt like I was ensconced in a museum.

The meal I like to remember is our luncheon at a French restaurant on Yugoslavia Street. Willie had reserved a table under old grapevines that not only shaded us from the sun but also surrounded us with a fresh green smell. An aged German actress, with long white hair, huge purple shawl and big hat, accompanied us. But it was not Ana, nor Willie, and especially not me, whom everybody looked at. It was Fred. At seventy-eight, he was blessed with a full head of white hair, erect posture and a regal attitude. He was dressed in tight gray slacks; a gray silk shirt with the top two buttons open exposing a white furry chest and a hot pink linen scarf draped around his shoulders, then knotted across his chest. His entrance was a Hollywood production. He paused when he entered the doorway and commanded the attention of the audience. Then, with grace and *noblesse oblige*, he strutted to our cozy table. I loved watching people look at him because he was beautiful to behold and he appeared to know it.

We discussed the gay community in Morocco.

Willie said, "We bought our house here about thirty years ago."

Fred said, "Twenty-eight!"

"We've a lot of friends from America and from the U.K. who also came about that time."

"We were here first," said Fred.

"Morocco accepted homosexuals when many parts of the world did not."

"I'm surprised," I said, "because I don't usually think of an Arabic country as liberal."

"For most things, they're not. When the French came in 1912 for the Protectorate, they brought a lot of sexual acceptance and the homosexual community followed."

Fred said, "It's harder for native Moroccan homosexuals, so, many of them marry and then maintain their other lives secretly."

During the weekend, we went out with other gay couples whom they had known for twenty-eight years. There seemed to be an international connection that was viable and supportive. One couple was Irish and the other British. Willie was fluent in French and said, "We've a lot of French friends too. It's easy for them to have a second home here because

French is a major second language and it's cheap for them too."

"Willie speaks French like a native."

"I'm not that good, Fred."

"I think you are," he said with a sly wink for Willie.

I hated to see the weekend end. I loved their American presence. I understood what they said. I didn't have to guess and they knew how to accept me. There were no hidden messages, frustrations, societal errors or insults. I had this interlude with my new friends and gained insight into my new country that I would not have gotten otherwise. Yet my resolve to stay away from the American community was still intact. I was determined to get to know Moroccans and to accept the changes that had to occur in me in order to adapt to Morocco. Each foray into my native community set me back in the integration process and assimilation into my new community. It had to come to an end, and my journey back on the airplane was a journey back into Morocco.

When I arrived at the airport in Fes, I ran into a fellow student from the Arabic Language School. She had never spoken to me before but I felt that she decided she could share a ride and tolerate an old lady in order to save a few dollars.

Celine said in her perfectly French accented English, "Would you like to share a taxi?" She was so icy in her invitation to share a ride that I felt inferior. Celine told me that she had an American mother and French father, had grown up in France, attended Harvard University, and planned to live in America.

I wanted to say no to the shared ride in the taxi because she was so haughty but I replied, "Love to, Christine."

"It's Celine," she said.

"Of course." I called her Christine every time she walked by me at school without saying hello.

We went outside and the taxi drivers wanted twenty dollars to drive us to the dormitory. That is a week's wages but we felt we had no choice. Suddenly a beautiful, young Moroccan woman said, "They are trying to cheat you. I will drive you where you want to go."

"I can't let you do that."

"It's okay."

"Really. We can pay that," I said.

She said, "I'm embarrassed that my countrymen are trying to cheat you. We Moroccans aren't like that." Her husband drove up and she commanded, "Get into the car."

First, she drove him home and then spent an additional fifteen minutes to chauffeur us to another side of the city where she dropped us at the school. I didn't know how to thank her but she said, "I don't want you to think badly of Moroccans." How could we after having witnessed such an unselfish act? I know I would never do this in America.

"*Shokrun,*" I smiled and waved.

Celine said something in French, which I couldn't understand, but she too smiled and stood there with me in the hot afternoon sun. The woman drove away and we never learned her name.

"*Au revoir,* Christine," I said as I hefted my green pack onto my back and headed back to the villa.

ROSH HASHANNAH AND YOM KIPPUR

The Jewish New Year approaches. On this holiday, 2000, it is Rosh Hashanah, 5761, a time to take inventory. This is one of the holiest days of the year and I am alone in Morocco. My whole family will celebrate without me. My husband will join me in November but for now all I have is the young Israeli woman Renat—we are joined at the hip.

We skip Arabic class to go to the Medina where she plans to give me the same tour she gives Israeli tourists when she works as a guide. We wind through the narrow streets of the Medina, which looks like Jerusalem's Old City. Everyone seems to know Renat when they enthusiastically yell, "Hi, Renat," or "Hi, Israeli." Their energy spills over to me so I smile and wave back like the Queen Mother, only I move more of my arm than just elbow to wrist. We visit the usual tourist stops but the highlight of the tour is the visit to the cemetery where a Jewish saint[*] is buried. She was beheaded after she refused to convert to Islam when the sultan's son wanted to marry her. Carved into her tomb is a niche where mourners light candles. The picture of candles in a saint's tomb doesn't seem so Jewish, but we do light candles and say *Kaddish*; Renat for her dead soldier friends and me for my parents. I know I am mourning for my parents but now I feel I am mourning for the rest of my life, for the life that is not here. I feel totally alone. I am highly emotional which makes me start to sob. Renat starts to cry too. We hold on to each other and I realize that now there is mist in the cemetery, our hair is soon peppered with globules of water, our faces are tear stained, my nose is runny and our hands black from the candles in the niche. Renat wipes her eyes with the side of her hand. Instantly, black is smeared from her right eye to her ear. I look

---

[*] Soleika Hachuel 1817-1834

at her brown curls like a Jewish Orphan Annie, brown eyes, toothy grin, fat cheeks, but now she has a black face. Soon our tears turn to howls of laughter. She is my sister.

As we leave the cemetery, a stall owner grabs Renat and bellows, "I'm Jewish too. I'm Soleika. My brothers live in Brooklyn but I can't leave my home in Fes." However, she does leave her stall unattended to walk with us. She bargains for our few purchases and introduces us to her friends in the Medina. She struts around in black high top tennis shoes, with us in tow because we are her family, the family who kisses her good-bye and then watches her go to collect her commissions.

In the Mellah, the old Jewish section, Renat takes me to the home where her father was born. The woman who now lives there spots Renat from the window and yells down to her in Arabic. Most of the women I have seen wear headscarves even in this hundred-degree heat; some tie these scarves tightly to their heads, wind the ends of the scarves into a rope and knot the rope on the top of their heads. Others wear them loose with the ends knotted under their chins. I am not sure what the significance of the different styles is, but this woman wears hers tied tightly around her head. A minute later she opens a door on street level and drags us up steep narrow steps into an apartment that is maybe one hundred square feet large with no kitchen and no visible door to a bathroom. It has one window. The King's picture is in the most prominent place while on the opposite wall is a lovely illuminated calligraphy from the Koran. On a small table sits a coffeepot next to a small bottle of gas that has a wire stand on top on which you can balance a pot in order to cook a meal. There is a butane lantern in the corner. There are no electric lights. She and Renat have an animated conversation while I stand there with my mute idiot smile. People try to include me in their conversations even though I have only a one hundred-word vocabulary. I usually nod my head like I understand, say "*nam*," or just smile. Renat is happy to see this woman because she always tells Renat stories about the family when it lived in this house. They kiss before we leave.

We walk around the Medina where the noise and smells are unique. Renat says, "Pay attention."

"I do, Renat. When I hear "*Balak*" I turn to see whether it's a cart or animal."

She pinches her nostrils, smiles at me and says, "No meat today."

As those words leave her mouth, we hear "*Balak!*" in front of us but I turn to see who is behind me as Renat screams, "Gloria!" In that one split second, as I turn, I see Renat's panicked face. I look behind me to realize that the foot that I have pivoted on has sunk into sickening, smelly dung. I turn back and look down at my red toenails as they sink along with my beautiful nubuck sandals. I cannot do anything to stop it. As I watch this millisecond process I think of my worries about the athlete's foot I have contracted since I use the shower at the villa. I think about my red sandals. I think about my polished toenails. I think about shit. The silence ends when three little boys scream something in Arabic. They run up close to me, turn, wave their hands and then run away while Renat stands there speechless. The noise of the Medina picks up. My right foot is in a fresh warm moist pile of dung. I know that the first thing I must do is lift this foot, which I cannot do because I do not want that foot to be part of me. But it is. I lift it. Suddenly, instead of sobs, Renat and I start to laugh. An Arabic woman comes up to me with a bucket of water and throws it on my foot. Another brings some newspaper. Suddenly the women in the Medina are helping me submerge my foot in water. I am amazed that the dung washes off so quickly. All of this happens while I am looking at the backs of the women's covered heads while they bend over to clean the contaminated foot. Renat never lets go of me. The miracle is that when my foot is removed from the sandal, the sandal washed and the foot washed, I am almost as good as new. I say, "*Shokrun,*" and the women smile, some with missing teeth, take their buckets, carry the newspaper, and go back to their business, expecting nothing for the deed they have just performed. We continue to walk towards the taxi stand.

We hurry to lunch at the home of my teacher, Nijia. She has asked me to bring Renat and another American Fulbright, Bianca, an Italian woman, who is the widow of an African American poet and is a naturalized American citizen now. Bianca has more street smarts and passion than I will ever have. I am envious of her. We talk openly about politics, sex, women's rights, abortion and I smile because it is so good to have close friends at this time. We are a *Havurah.*[*]

Nijia's apartment is beautiful, with two huge Moroccan salons or living rooms. Both have narrow couches that line the walls with round tables, a little higher than American coffee tables, in the center of the room. These tables are pulled to a corner when there is a meal; low stools are brought in and half the diners lounge on these couches and half sit on the stools. Nijia is about forty-five. She is fluent in English and French and is knowledgeable about American culture. She and her husband are both professors at the university.

"I've been to the States," she boasts with a proud smile.

"California?" I ask.

"Not yet."

"Put it on your list as the next place to go so you can stay with me."

Her maid cooks couscous every Friday because Nijia said, "I never learned how and, besides, it is too much trouble." She pays her maid six dollars a day to clean. Nijia is very modern in her attitude and clearly sees the problems of her country even though she loves it dearly. The poverty is constant, health care minimal, and unemployment an epidemic. Because there are no social services for the handicapped, she

---

[*] Hebrew for group of friends

and a friend have started a charity that gives wheelchairs to poor Moroccans. They have received over fifty wheelchairs donated from individuals in the United States and have given them to the needy.

"We interview everyone who wants a wheelchair."

"Are there a lot of applicants?"

"Thousands. The reason you don't see handicapped people on the street here is because they have no mobility. They can't get around."

"What do they do?"

"They sit in the house until they die." She adds, "My maid. When she quits work, she'll have no money."

After delicious couscous, we hurry home and rush to the synagogue with big smiles in spite of our lateness for services. We feel unholy and pressured. Maybe this is an unwritten part of the Jewish holiday celebration, only tonight we wear no beautiful clothing, no jewelry, and there are no tickets, no guards, no late services and no assigned seats. We find the unmarked synagogue above a store. The steep steps lead to two passageways where the women are steered to the right into a curtained hall with two rows of older women who are sitting and staring at the curtain. There is atonal noise coming from the other side of the curtain but it is unchoreographed and unidentifiable. The opaque curtain blocks everything. We smile at our friend Soleika whose white hair is such a contrast to the henna color of most Moroccan women. She looks lovely without her baseball cap. I have forgotten my glasses but notice there is a woman dressed all in white with some kind of hat that has a white bird nesting on her head. I make a note to get close to her after services so that I can see what it really is. Almost all of the women are bareheaded, which is so different from most of the Moroccan women who wear scarves. I am not sure whether their beauty surrounds them or whether I find them beautiful because they are Jewish and the synagogue is a comfortable place for me.

Suddenly, I hear feet shuffle. The service is over. The women wait until the men have filed down the steps. As we descend the steep steps, I am aware of the contrast in shoe sounds as I listen to the sound of the Moroccan shoes on each step compared to the silence of the Teva sandals that the Israelis wear.

We talk to some Israelis outside who invite us, Renat, Astrid, my Christian German friend, and Harriet, a Ph.D. student from the University of Massachusetts, to join them for dinner at the Golden Rain Restaurant. As soon as we sit down, they whisk out apples, pomegranates and honey. A bottle of wine appears and in unison we stand and sing the *Kiddush*; then a woman named Tamar lights candles. When we chant the *Shehecheyanu*, we tighten our circle as each word of Hebrew is sung. The patrons in the restaurant have become quiet and I watch them watch us. Suddenly as we finish, they start to yell, "*Shabbat Shalom* Jews! Rosh Hashanah Jews! Jews!" I think I am drunk because we are being applauded and toasted. We smile and each of us squeezes the hands of whoever is next to us. Then Renat and I start to cry. I remember my cousin said, "You pinch a Jew in Tel Aviv and a Jew in New York says 'Ouch'!" Our nerve endings are connected. The picture of us is like a Fellini movie because half of us do not speak Hebrew, others do not speak English and Astrid speaks German while Renat and I laugh as tears trail down our faces. Yet, we have a three-hour dinner talking about our uniqueness, our love for each other, and our luck finding this group in an Arab country this New Year, 5761.

Sunday morning I wake at 5:00 to catch a bus back to Tetouan/Martil. I am now ready to leave the school and make my way in the academic world of Morocco. I must prepare my lectures for the new semester. I hate to leave my friends at the villa but must begin at the university. Quietly, I pack up my things and go downstairs to have a cup of tea.

Michal, the German boy who lives with Holocaust guilt and a bird tattoo, tiptoes into the kitchen and says, "Gloria, have a good time but hurry back because we are your family." I rub his shaved head affectionately.

He sits down as Renat comes in and says, "I'm going to the bus station."

Then Jeremy enters, winks and says, "So, Babe, you're off to the real world. Knock 'em dead." He has recovered from having his wallet stolen yesterday.

Astrid tiptoes in and whispers, "Please write me," as she puts her address in my pocket. I never could find the little piece of paper.

Sila, a handsome Pakistani-American Fulbright student, who had moved out a week ago but unbeknownst to me, returned last night so he could be sure to say good-bye, nonchalantly leans against the stove. Finally, the maid and the night guard creep in wearing their nightclothes. Now everyone in the house is in the eight by eight kitchen that is filled with good-byes and tears. Sila and Hamid both hug me even though they had warned me that, as devout Moslems, they would never be able to touch me.

Renat and I sit at the station and hold hands until my bus comes. She complains that her bankcard is not working. As I get on the bus, I put a $100 bill in her hand. I throw her a kiss and wonder what her last name is.

Back in my Martil home, there is not a single window with a light on at night in my deserted neighborhood and I am terrified.

My television transmits only Arab TV and sometime during the week I see pictures of burned American and Israeli flags, dead Jews and dead Palestinians. There are no American newspapers and I am unable to reach the US. This is something horrible but I don't know what it is and can ask no one. There is a war somewhere and I think it is the Middle East, but I do not know definitely what or where. My parents had a mantra by which they measured every news article: "Is it good for the Jews or is it bad for the Jews?" I feel this is definitely bad for the Jews.

Thursday, at the cyber café, there is a warning from Damon Paulson at the Fulbright office in Rabat. I copy part of it and try to print it up just because the words are so frightening. I read the words over and over and over again:

To all US grantees still in country,
 The following message was received by my office today. These announcements are fairly standard procedure when there are perceived possible threats against Americans or American interests in the region. The message, I believe is no cause for panic or making major changes of plans. The wording of the announcement (i.e., "individuals may be planning terrorist activities against U.S. interests in Morocco") does not suggest any widespread danger, but rather the theoretical (read: distant) possibility of a single attack on a prominent target. Nevertheless, it would be a good idea to exercise a bit more caution than usual in line with the recommendations outlined in the announcement below.
Regards,
Damon

PUBLIC ANNOUNCEMENT, U.S. DEPARTMENT OF STATE
Office of the Spokesman, Morocco
The U.S. Government has information that has not yet been determined to be credible that individuals may be planning terrorist activities against U.S. interests in Morocco. Some U.S. Government personnel who were temporarily in Morocco have left the country.
In accordance with the previous Worldwide Caution, U.S. citizens are urged to maintain a high level of vigilance and to

take appropriate steps to increase their security awareness to reduce their vulnerability. Americans should maintain a low profile, avoid crowds, and vary routes and times for all required travel. All Americans in Morocco are advised to register with the U.S. Consulate General in Casablanca and to consult the Consulate General for updated safety and security information....

I decide to return to Fes for Yom Kippur so I can ask Renat about what this is. On Friday morning I leave at 10 A.M. Five hours later, I arrive in Fes. I walk back to the sanctuary of the villa and push myself against the white walls that line the streets in an effort to be in the shade. Familiar faces and houses without winter shutters greet me. People are out and about on the hot pavement and stores are busy. Renat and I scream like twelve-year-olds when we see each other.

Hans, Hamid, Michal, Nora, Bianca, Astrid, Renat and I go to dinner. The worst part of the whole day is when I learn that tomorrow, my good friends Hamid, Nora and Bianca plan to protest the Intifada in Israel. It has nothing to do with me, they say, but has to do with their opposition to the policies of Israel.

Bianca says, "I grew up in an Italian communist family. We always root for the underdog." I see that her hair (which she says she tints because it turned white after her husband died), her skin, and her eyes are all the same brown color. She looks like toast. Her words turn me to ice, yet she looks so warm. The feelings and the vision confuse me because I have never been in a situation like this in my sixty plus years.

She doesn't answer me when I ask, "Were you on the side of the Jews when the Jews were the underdogs?"

They say they have nothing against Renat and me. The three Germans (Hans, Michal and Astrid) push their food around on their plates and remain quiet. They understand. These are familiar words.

Bianca spends the night with us in Renat's room as we had planned for my visit. All night I watch her sleep.

The next day the three of us go to the odorous Medina. Last time they yelled to Renat, "Hello Israeli!" but this time it isn't a friendly greeting. They shout at her and also at me. "Jew!" "*Shalom!*" which has become an epithet for "Israeli." Now, instead of waves, they stand up and show raised fists at the end of their extended straight tan arms.

Bianca says, "Don't tell anyone you're from the United States. It's dangerous." I say over and over, "I am Canadian. I am from beautiful British Columbia." Renat joins the litany. Now we are both Canadians.

Bianca walks in front of us the whole time. It is crowded and difficult to walk three abreast, but even if I drop back behind Renat, Bianca does not join her. She separates herself from us both physically and emotionally. I watch her bony back, looking for clues. Renat and I are the vacant-eyed observers now. Bianca says, "Shhh. Don't talk to anyone. Don't even talk to each other." I know we are repulsive to her. She knows I hate the meat section, but she leads us through it anyway. Bile is collecting at the back of my throat and I feel as if I am swallowing vomit. Bianca leads us to the taxi stand and leaves us after she whispers to me, "Don't tell anyone you're Jewish." Her good-bye is a nod, and in spite of the inescapable sun, I am cold.

At 8:00 P.M. we take a taxi to go to a produce stand. The taxi driver, who wears a white knitted skullcap that looks like a *yarmulke*, drives us to a busy part of town. I sit in back and listen to Renat and the driver speak in Arabic. She talks about France and I am not sure what he says. Whenever I ask a question, she motions me to be quiet. He waits for us to buy our vegetables. The small produce stands are crowded because it is always busy in Fes. We return to the taxi with five large, heavy bags of fruit and vegetables. We get out of the taxi with our load about three blocks away from the villa. I start to protest but Renat leans close to me and mutters, "He wanted to kill all the Jews. He recognized my Hebrew accent but I said I wasn't Israeli. I told him that I am a French Canadian immigrant who was born in Fes at my father's address."

"That's horrible, Renat." I move closer to her for protection. She leans into me with all the vegetables slammed into my belly.

I get more worried every minute. I don't know if I look Jewish or not, but people yell *shalom* at me when I walk behind Renat and I look at them as if they are crazy. Maybe she looks Jewish. Maybe I look Jewish.

I can understand the people of Morocco and their mass protests. Arabs are getting killed. However, I cannot understand Hamid from Tulsa, Nora from Virginia, and Bianca from Italy, who now will march against us. It is isolating and excruciatingly painful.

Renat needs to pick up some money from a friend at the Mendes hotel because her bankcard is useless. For protection, she appeals to Hans: "Come with us to the Mendes Hotel."

He has terrible diarrhea but responds; "I'd like to go, Renat, as long as it won't take too long." He is a bad liar.

"Hans, you bargain with the driver."

He asks the driver, "How much?"

"Twenty dirham."

"Twenty-five for a round trip."

"Get in." And so we do.

Hans gets in front while Renat and I silently sit in the back seat with our hands clasped tightly together. She wants no one to hear her accent. I want to disappear. We are both scared.

The television images are horrible, rife with dead bodies strewn everywhere in the West Bank and Gaza Strip. Harriet told me, "Don't believe Arab television. These horrible pictures could be from other wars or even staged." But there is a war; an Intifada rages between Israelis and Palestinians. The uprising is not just a protest; it is violent and escalates to all areas of Israel and the Palestinian regions. The violence has spread through the Arab world like the plague. Suddenly, neither Renat nor I feel safe and I think Hans does not feel safe when he is with us. He chews his thumbnail. This is the real thing and we are the closest target. Renat is smaller than I am but, for me, she is my strength, my protector and we hold hands whenever we can. Maybe she is used to being strong or maybe she is leaning close to me so I can protect her. But I cannot protect anyone. I am scared to death. Our bare arms stick together from perspiration. The money transaction and round trip take thirty-five minutes.

The next day is *Kol Nidre*. Renat was up all night with stomach pains and looks dreadful. "I'm too sick to do anything. I'm going to bed."

"Does that mean you're not the chef?"

She smiles at my sick humor.

"I don't want to cook," I whine. "That damn stove is about to blow me to Mecca."

She gets into bed and whispers, "Go across the street from the post office. There's a place that sells chickens."

"What does this place look like?"

She closes her eyes without an answer.

I wend my way to the post office and the search begins. It is impossible to tell a restaurant from any other business unless it has tables outside, but here only half the restaurants have outdoor tables. I go into every café and bar where I ask if they have a whole cooked chicken and since I don't know the word for chicken, I flap my arms wildly and crow a rooster's "cock-a-doodle do." They tell me the word is "*jeeje*" but the next restaurateur does not understand my Arabic, so I do the chicken routine again. Sweat pours down my back and my thighs are grinding together because of the heat. I feel like I am in a constant spasm but now I am sure that I have fever because I am so hot. I walk up and down Rue Hassan Deux for fifteen or twenty minutes; still no luck. A young woman stops me and says she is studying English. I know this because the only two words I understand are English and teacher. We have a pitiful exchange of words; however, she does supply me with directions that lead me to a chicken farmer's store. He has cages of live chickens. I try to explain that I need a dead chicken. He does not understand. No one understands me. I am a lunatic who runs around the streets and impersonates a chicken. Striving to reach my goal, I add another step to my pantomime. I flap my wings, say "cock-a-doodle-do," slit my throat, close my eyes and drop my head to the side to signify that I want a dead chicken.

Finally, after ten people have responded negatively to my question, I meet a young man who understands a little English. "Mohammed, I need a whole cooked dead chicken." (I've learned that it's polite to address a male stranger as Mohammed.) He nods and takes me to Café Milano where there is neither a dead nor live chicken in sight and he leaves me. I tell the waiter that I want to buy a whole dead chicken, cooked. He understands me and leaves for ten minutes, and then returns with one piece of chicken on top of French fries. I instruct him again and finally after one-and-a-half hours of back and forth plus two programs on Arab TV, I have two pieces of cooked dead chicken, one slice of bread, and no potatoes.

Harriet joins Renat, Hans, and me for dinner. I plant two candles in melted wax on the burned bottom of a frying pan and chant the blessing for *Yom Tov*. Renat is really sick and is bent over the table while we eat. On her plate is a tiny piece of chicken, which goes untouched. I look at this pathetic scene in front of me—a sheet for the tablecloth, four oddly patterned dishes are the ersatz china, two glasses and two cups are for beverages, two pieces of cooked dead chicken, one chopped cucumber, and green beans complete the meal. This is the *erev* Yom Kippur feast. This is my *Kol Nidre*. I don't know how I feel except that it is a new feeling and one that I cannot describe. It veers from fear to joy, from loneliness to isolation, then from nothingness to completeness.

I grab Renat's hand under the table. She is hot. "I took some medicine," and then she tells me the Hebrew name, which means nothing to me. Harriet and I make small talk, Hans says nothing, and Renat moans. Harriet takes out a bottle of huge pills. Nonchalantly, she says, "These are chemotherapy for my cancer." I watch her thin lips, gold nose ring that protrudes from her tiny right nostril, blonde hair pulled into a bun, and cool thirty-year-old face as she explains the regimen she is on. Below her translucent skin, I envision the grains of chemo as they rush to fight the explosion of cancer cells. The sound of pumped blood deafens me.

Hans watches all of us while he neatly arranges the green beans in a row on his plate. Again, I want to vomit from the nauseous feelings of helplessness and fear that is ever present.

We decide that Renat cannot walk to the synagogue. I say, "Stay home, Renat," but she shakes her head and says, "No, no. I can't miss *Kol Nidre*." Little blonde Harriet, all one hundred pounds of her, who before had appeared strong, now seems so vulnerable when she stands in the middle of the street as she tries to stop a taxi.

In the taxi, I say to Harriet, "The pictures on television are horrible. I am petrified. The Intifada looks like World War II."

Harriet answers, "Don't believe the news. You don't know where the pictures are from, when they were taken, or even if they're actors. News is beamed in from Qatar and Saudi Arabia. It's propaganda. Don't believe anything. They lie."

"I feel so naive." We continue the ride in deafening silence.

We go to the area of the other Fes synagogue but we haven't told the taxi driver exactly where we are going, so

Harriet directs in French, "Go two blocks to the left. Now go right. Now go straight two blocks and then left. Stop!"

We walk for a couple of blocks when I realize that the stores are all closed and there is no traffic. I have been told that there is a soccer game tonight but no one is out. For the first time since I arrived in Fes, the cafés are silent. We arrive at a place where a police van blocks the street at the corner and there are policemen positioned in a line down the middle of the street. Harriet talks to them while I support Renat. They let us pass and Renat crawls up the steps while we walk up the steep flight to the second-floor synagogue.

The women are even higher on a side balcony, but unlike last week, these beige curtains are open. Three women have *makhzurs* and the rest of us just sit and watch the tops of the men's heads. In spite of the white walls and white ceiling, it feels dark in the synagogue. The tunes and the physical surroundings are alien, and the people do not look like me, yet I am home. I hear an occasional amen or *Adonai* but I don't even recognize the *Kaddish*, which I know by heart in Ashkenazi Hebrew.

I look at the ceiling because it is directly in front of me, where I count nineteen chandeliers. Two or three are the same design but they are scattered at random and each has different kinds of crystal or light bulbs, as if they represent a different year or the diverse tastes of various building committees. There is no order. I look out the window at the deserted street when, suddenly, I see lights from a car. I wonder why there is traffic now. I evaluate my position. I am behind a stone partition up to my chest, close to the window. I wonder where the bomb will hit when it is thrown through the window. Will the partition shield me from flying glass or shrapnel?

There are two fragile children who innocently play in front of the window and I want to scream, "Move! Get away from that window! Damn it, run!" However, there is no voice. I gasp. I have no language; so I pray like crazy. The inability to communicate restrains my body, but my mind is deliriously visiting the chambers of persecution horror. Suddenly, it is quiet. I open my eyes to see there are six men entering the synagogue. Three are in *jallabahs*, yellow slippers with pointed toes, fez hats, two are in military uniforms that have four stars on each shoulder, and the sixth has on a dark European style business suit. They quietly sit down. They are a bit darker complexioned than the Jews in the synagogue, maybe a little shorter. Two men at the reading table begin to *daven* with the words Mohammed, Hassan, and *enshallah*, ("if Allah wills it,") embedded in the prayer. Everyone stands for a moment of silence. Prayers resume and the latecomers leave. I learn that they were the mayor of Fes, representatives of the king, and two generals. The king's representatives and mayor have brought reassurances from the king for his Jews' safety. They have received blessings and silence has been observed for all who have died in the Intifada.

Soon, services are over. We adjourn to the outside where we quietly watch the police guard observe us as we blend with the pedestrians of Fes on the other side of the barricade. It is Yom Kippur 5761, a time of great unrest and fear. I am alone and yet I am not alone. I have prayed harder than at any other time of my life because I am so frightened. Oh my God, please give us peace and life. Amen.

ALONE IN MARTIL

When is man strong until he feels alone?
—Robert Browning

The house in Martil is no home. It is a cell. It is a prison. Physically, I can describe it as lovely. The fountain in the front patio is beautiful but was turned off when the owners left for the winter. There is no life on this street whose name I have yet to learn. I am afraid to go out in the dark, which is a real impediment to my daily life since it gets dark so early now. The kitchen is downstairs where two huge black roaches, the size of mice, run around in search for whatever they can find. There is no bug spray anywhere upstairs in the other rooms. My yogurt is in the refrigerator downstairs but, luckily, I have a box of Tootsie Pops that I brought to give to the children here. I eat four of them for dinner. The orange ones are the best with green a close second.

There are no towels and I am happy that I thought to steal one from a hotel in Fes.

There is no telephone in the house and for some reason my cell phone is dead. I hope that I am able to find a shop to fix it. Perhaps it is a battery or maybe it is just my bad luck. The television has only one channel and that is Arabic. I leave it on because I find the noise is soothing tonight. I only brought six cassettes with me and since my arrival, I realize that I have listened to them a dozen times and also realize that I have chosen well. I will find a music store and a phone store tomorrow in addition to the various necessities on the list that forms my purpose for tomorrow.

At 8:10 I realize that I must go to bed or I will get more depressed. I am afraid to try to fall asleep in this new house. I have not taken a sleeping pill since the flight over, so it is time to have a good night's sleep. I grab my nightgown and go into the bathroom. I need to take a shower. Here, to take a shower is a lovely custom because one sits relaxed in the bathtub while holding the hand shower that distributes water all over. I sit there and continue to put hot water on my dejected body until the hot water runs out. That is my signal to get up and dry myself. The bathroom feels like a steam room, which makes it easy to pretend that I am somewhere else, far away, as I begin to relax. Since I forgot to bring up a glass or bottled water, I take one half of an *Ambien* with a slurp of water from the sink faucet. Within fifteen minutes I am mercifully asleep.

Morning brings light but not a good mood. I know that I need to get out while it is daytime. Still afraid to go downstairs, I eschew breakfast and set out to find a coffee shop and internet café so I can e-mail everyone how wonderful Morocco is.

My street, which I later learn is called Rue Casablanca, is a short, one-block street that has three-story apartments and one blue eight-foot square metal shed that is a grocery. Nestled in the middle of this block is one private home that shares walls with apartment buildings that dwarf it on each side. The front yard has a white stone fence that lines a concrete patio. This is where I live. One end of the street intersects with the beach and the beautiful Mediterranean Sea; the other leads to the business area but most of the stores have blue metal shutters, similar to garage doors, pulled down and padlocked for the winter. I have no idea what kinds of stores exist behind these metal obstructions, but, whatever they are, they are hidden. Luckily, the grocery store is open as is a small café across the street. Other than that, I live on an abandoned street in an abandoned neighborhood.

I can see the sea from my front door. I walk towards the magnetic blue and am hypnotized. It is such a vivid color that if I saw a photo of this vision, I would say that the film distorted the colors. The sand is an endless bank of white crystals warmed by a slight breeze. I start to feel good, a sensation that is new and welcome. A few people are out on the beach and I watch them as they walk, look, stand and breathe. I wonder where they come from. This site is magnificent and were it not for my desolate aloneness, I would sit all day. I walk about nine blocks until, finally, I find a small business section that is composed of small one-story white stucco buildings on a courtyard facing the sea. Here there are two Internet cafes but they have only French or Arabic keyboards. Coincidentally, they are not connected to the Internet because the lines are down, which does not surprise me. In fractured French, I ask the attendant, "*Où est le taxi pour Tetouan?* He walks out the front door and points across the street where there is a group of people and a small bench. "*Shokrun.*" My sad lips mouth the Arabic words as I walk out into the blinding sun.

Twenty minutes later I am in the center of Tetouan where I try to find landmarks so I will be able to get a taxi back to Martil. Tetouan is a lovely Mediterranean town with a big square in the center. The white stucco buildings are two stories high with wrought iron porches on the second floor. Large archways form the front of the buildings and there is a grand Catholic church that no longer holds services but hosts the Cervantes Instituto for Spanish Language. In the center of the square is a parkway with gigantic palm trees. It is now eleven o'clock and soon there will be the lunchtime break so I know that I have to hurry.

The first store that looks like fun is a stationery boutique that seems to have newspapers from every country. I am lucky because the *International Herald Tribune* is only five days old. This will keep me busy for an hour when all the stores close. Street merchants have blankets in front of the shops where they have mounds of merchandise pyramided at least one foot high. A man hawks cell phone cases for twenty dirhams, a little less than two dollars. I bargain with him and buy a case for a dollar fifty. The close of the sale gives me a rush that lets me know that I am alive and can react to something. A feeling of well being creeps into my limp ego.

I walk into a perfumery and for the first time in days I see a woman with makeup. I smell the perfumes and lotions. She smiles at me. The only thing I can manage to say is "*Je ne parle francais*," and I motion to my eyebrows because I notice that hers are tweezed very thin. She points to me and says, "*Vous*?" I have no confidence in my ability to be understood so I draw an eyebrow with a tweezers. She points to her watch that shows 11:55. She holds up five fingers and I think she says in Arabic that she will take me somewhere at noon.

Sure enough, five minutes later, the young woman locks the shop, grabs my arm, and walks me about five blocks away and up three flights of unlit stairs to a big brown wooden door without a sign or any other identifying information. She rings the bell. While we wait for an answer, my imagination suddenly sees naive me in this dark hall while people rob me. I start to hyperventilate and lean over to catch my breath when a tall woman in a white uniform answers the door. She takes my hand while I turn to thank the shop woman who has run down the steps. She escorts me in to a clean, clinic-like spa that has three closed doors surrounding a reception desk. The woman, named Saadia, steers me into a small room that has a long massage table, and a heavenly variety of creams, waxes, towels, soaps and ointments. Saadia is a sad-eyed esthetician who waxes my eyebrows and a masseuse who gives me an incredibly wonderful massage. Two hours later I pay her ten dollars. She is very happy with her two-dollar tip and I am ecstatic with the exhilarating energy my body finally has.

Nearby is a small sandwich shop on Rue 10 Avril called the New York Café, where I sit down for a wonderful vegetable sandwich and a Coca-Cola Light while I read a week old "International Herald Tribune." It is terribly hot but I am dressed in all cotton clothing plus my red sandals that are perfect for long walks. Tomorrow I will go to the university and tonight will be the same as last night, only now I save a new crossword puzzle for the evening. En route to the taxi stand, I find a cyber café that has an English keyboard and for two hours I write everyone in America that I am well, have a beautiful home and have spent the day at a spa. It is easy to sound upbeat and I hope that no one worries. It is like eating an elephant; you can only take one bite at a time.

I feel so good about my eyebrow arch and massage that on the way home I decide to get my hair washed. I find a little shop on Miramar Street, about two blocks from my house, where a pretty woman sits outside and prays for a customer. The name of the salon is *Le Ritz,* so I decide it must be good. She washes my hair in cool water and uses no shampoo. I am not sure whether I am supposed to bring my own or if she is afraid I will not pay an extra fee for shampoo. I silently watch her pick up a dirty brush when she turns on the hand-held dryer. For four dollars she washes and blows my hair dry. She gets a one-dollar tip, so now we are both happy.

When I enter the house, I realize that it is no different than it was last night and I sink into a black hole. I can talk to no one from Thursday noon until next Tuesday. I want to ask Jamel where all his friends are but I know I would yell at him if we ever discussed the lie. There is no one here to bond with but the devil. I am so angry with Jamel because he insisted that I take this rental. I knew it was a mistake from the start, which is why I told the owners I would rent it for only a month. I am so isolated here.

I decide that I am going to move out as soon as I can and, suddenly, I am filled with boundless energy. There is a little voice in my head that blames me, not Jamel, for the lease. Defiantly I pack up everything except my pajamas and another outfit. I am ready to move. I don't know where, but now the victim in me feels good for this new decision. My depression is lifting like a theater curtain. For the first time in weeks I feel that this might work out because I have taken charge. Some unknown power now fuels my sluggish engine.

I sleep like the dead. However, the next day a spurt of energy accompanies me for a fresh baguette and then to the Internet café where I learn about the death of my dear friend Libby Fain. For two days I cut myself off from everyone and everything. There is not much to eliminate from my life, but what little there is must be eliminated. The few people I know cannot help me here.

Mourning is a lonely activity but when you are alone, you mourn for the departed and you mourn for yourself. My beautiful friend, Libby Winer Fain, died after a valiant fight against a horrible, rare progressive disease. I was so far away. There was no one to hug me; no one to hold me; and no one to know the pain I was in. Libby's pain was over and her loved ones mourned together, prayed together, and lamented the loss together. I could only say *Kaddish*• alone. I could only cry alone. I could only remember alone.

I read once, although I don't remember where, "Of all the pains of all the prisoners, mine is the hardest to bear," and when I sat down to write her daughter, I think I was aware of her pain, for she too was alone and her pain was the hardest to bear.

Dearest Sally-Ann,

For the past few weeks all I have thought of is my beautiful Libby and now, how sad we are that her star is no longer shining. She has left her light everywhere she has been. I know you will receive reams of letters from all the people whose lives she touched and they will focus on the years of glory. I was a witness to a few of those years but it was of the subsequent years that I was truly participatory.

_____

• Kaddish is the Jewish prayer a mourner chants that extols the glory of the Lord even while devastated by the loss of a dear one.

I remember when I called your mother the first Sunday she, newly widowed, had returned from Switzerland. We made small talk peppered with inane niceties. She thanked me for the call. I phoned her the next Sunday and again we spoke. Needless to say, our conversations continued and our friendship bloomed. She had a keen intellect, an insatiable curiosity and a love of life. She was blessed and was happiest when she shared her blessings with those around her.

When she was at our house for a Seder, she fell down our front step and that was the first of the falls I witnessed. She was up, and ready to go on. But the big fall at your house was the beginning of our affair. If you remember, we sat in the bedroom with her while a bag of frozen peas was perched on her stitched forehead. We watched Cal Ripken play baseball. Other people may have been with her in more elegant settings but I cannot believe they had more fun. The next day she turned purple. Yet, that night she went to the symphony. When I saw her doctor, I said, "Bill, Libby went to the symphony opening with a purple face," and he said, "I hope she didn't tell anyone I'm her doctor!" This symphony was the first of Libby's most difficult triumphs. Little could stop her participatory personality from its usual involvement. Although it was the beginning of the horrible illness that finally took her from us, it was also the beginning of a valiant struggle to be a part of this beautiful world and to savor every moment. She attended and hosted Libby Fain signature events until the end. No one could throw a party like Libby.

Your mother made her "dying" a part of her living. We knew she wanted us to remember her last few years as living and not dying. She made sure we laughed (Remember the ice cream sandwich on her face!) and she made sure she knew what was happening in the world. When I called her, she wouldn't talk about herself but only asked about my kids, what I was doing, and what was current. She was interested in what my life was and she listened to my problems and my concerns.

She reassured me and helped me put so much into perspective. She gave me hope.

One morning while you were asleep, she and I talked. She told me about the house in Mexico and how your Dad got the mariachi band to serenade her the night she moved in. She talked about how romantic he was and how their life together was magical. She paused and looked up. I think she heard the music.

Sally-Ann, we both knew Libby—with the sunhat as big as an umbrella—was beautiful, intelligent, clever, fun, generous, silly, unpredictable and fiercely loyal. We knew she was blessed and realized it. How lucky we all were to have had a part of her.

There is never a good time or way to lose a parent. We can always think of one more thing we want to say, one more question we want to ask, or one more minute we want to have, but we know your beautiful mother was ready to leave. She gave each of us a piece of herself so that what is good in us will remind us of her; what is generous in us will remind us of her; what is spiritual in us will remind us of her; and when we eat crusty bread and baked garlic, it will remind us of her. I know I will never look at a purple flower or any thing of beauty without thoughts of her for they will forever be Libby. We will see her everywhere.

I am sure that she did not see a white light at the end. I know she saw a tall man with a bow tie who beckoned her to come dance with him. Your beautiful mother has escaped the body that betrayed her. Now she is free to move around at her own calling. There can be no perfect world without Libby in it but let us never forget her. Her memory is a blessing.

I wish I were there with you. I love you and I loved your Mother. My time with her was a gift, a treasure I will always revisit in my heart and in my memory. We will miss her too. Please extend our sympathy to your dear brothers, husband, sisters-in-law and all who loved her and now mourn her passing. The world is a sadder place today.

Love, Gloria

I wrote the letter and it didn't make me feel any better. I went for a walk about three o'clock when Morocco was ablaze. Very few people had re-emerged from the afternoon siesta. I looked for something familiar, a face, a place, a synagogue, some sort of refuge, but found none.

I finally went to the sea. Here the aquamarine water softened the blast of the sun. There were only a few people out, so I sat down on a bench and stared at the water. The waves hypnotized me and my heart beat in rhythm with the surf. It was noisy and yet desolate because of the absence of people. The warm void spoke to me, reassured me, and comforted me. There was no other place to go or be.

I picked up a sandwich for dinner and returned to my house. I listened to "Madame Butterfly" and as it came to the humming chorus when the ship pulled into port, I relaxed. This was my salvation. I hummed the melody, internalized the music, and tried to push the sadness away. It was the beginning of a lesson on how to heal myself, for I mourned the loss of myself too.

IN MEMORY OF YOSEF AVRAHAMI AND VADIM NORZHICH

For four weeks in October, Martil was my home. I tried to set up a workable routine to fight off culture shock, the very thing I teach at U.C. Berkeley. My ESL students in America go through it, so I know what it is and I know it is necessary to experience it before you integrate into a foreign community. However, the academic knowledge does not lessen the pain of entry. It still hurts and there is disorientation and depression. I fight the depression and try to distinguish between depression and being lonely and alone. I set up a routine that is amazingly pleasant and I find that I can go a whole day, twenty-four hours, without speaking to anyone in complete sentences. I walk a lot. I look at the sea. I send e-mail twice a day and I regulate my vegetarian diet.

The first day I went to a local sandwich shop. I was excited about the challenge of pointing to various foods that were displayed in two-quart unrefrigerated clear glass bowls. I tried to convey the message that in my sandwich I did not want the sausage, mayonnaise, eggs, or French fries. In fractured French, Arabic, and by hand gestures, I showed the sandwich maker that I wanted cheese, lettuce, tomatoes, onions, beets, green peppers, mustard, and pickles. I ordered my Coca-Cola Light and sat down. About five minutes later, the manager, sandwich maker and waiter approached my table with what they thought I had ordered. I didn't think I could do better a second time so I applauded their success and ate a rice sandwich with mustard.

There were good days and bad days during the month I lived in Martil. At first, when I went to a café or a coffee shop, I sat in front or outside where Moroccan women never sat. The only women who occupied these seats were foreigners and prostitutes. After ten days, I realized that I didn't need to prove my independence and that to sit in back with the Moroccan women took the edge off my foreignness.

On hectic school days, I loved to go to the *Minzah Salon de Thé* for a few solitary hours between classes, away from colleagues and students. It was near the only Catholic Church in Martil located on Los Cruces Street in the old section that had narrow streets, laundry blowing in the hot breeze, and noisy children in white school uniforms playing in the street. The men in the café sat here all day because there was nothing else for them to do. They had no jobs and hobby was a non-existent word. However, they did have camaraderie and I loved to observe their expressive faces when they were happy, angry or relaxed. They spoke loudly, flailed their hands and touched each other when they talked. They also kissed each other's cheeks when they met or departed. Moroccans have a wonderful tradition in the way they amplify a handshake. They shake your right hand and immediately touch their chest to show you that their affection for you comes directly from the heart.

The best scenario was during the soccer or football games on TV. I had no idea what they said to each other or what they yelled, but these men would jump up, sit down, take a sip of coffee, jump up, take a puff of cigarette, sit down, yell, move a checker, throw the dice, yell and repeat the cycle. They were participants, not spectators. The lone ones, however, seemed as if they were in a trance and it appeared that, in order to participate in this spectator game, you needed a partner.

One day, I sat in back of the café and graded papers as I nursed a café au lait. It was hot but I found if I barely moved, my body temperature seemed to go down. I smiled as I heard the sudden wild cheers from the men. I knew there had been a goal. The noise continued until finally it sounded like pandemonium, so I raised my eyes and saw the television screen. There was a strange picture. There was no game but there was a crowd.

Framed by a window, a dark man displayed the palms of his hands that were covered in red paint. He waved his hands vigorously. A tall man immediately in front of me stood up so I couldn't see the screen, but the noise continued to get louder. I did not hear all of the sounds but I felt the bedlam and chaos.

I could no longer act disinterested. I stood up and moved to the right of the tall man where I could see that all the men in the café were upright. Even the ubiquitous cat was attentive.* The only other woman in the rear of the café remained seated, self-involved while she continued to drink her mint tea. She had never made eye contact with anyone in the café. The backgammon players had stopped, hypnotized by the TV. Cigarettes were parked in ashtrays as the men shouted as if we were part of the bleacher gang, the spectators, and something unusual was in process. Only this was not a game. This was not a competition. The man with one eye had his head turned at a funny angle and I knew that he was watching the monitor with his good eye while the blind eye stared vacantly, unmoving and upward toward the dangling light bulb. The noise, the rumble, was deafening so that it was impossible to identify words. The smell of bodies increased with the smell of smoke, coffee, and heat.

Suddenly, I realized that the hands weren't covered in paint. It was blood. Then a body was flung out the window and there was a roar from the TV, or maybe now it was from the café. I didn't know. It bombarded me from all sides and made me feel like I was being swallowed by a wave of noise. I couldn't determine where the sounds were coming from. But there was blood, lots of noise, and a flying soldier launched out

---

* Renat told me that the Koran mentions cats so Moroccans have many cats and treat them royally as opposed to dogs that are abused and are seldom house pets. Restaurants, stores and even the schools have cats everywhere.

the window.* I recognized the pronunciation *"Ees-rah-ay-li"* and I knew the airborne man was an Israeli. My mind became a kaleidoscope of the TV, the blind eye, the smoke, a man soaring through the air, thundering sounds, finger-paint, sirens, a flying soldier.

Jewish blood had caused the commotion and Jewish blood propelled me out of the café where I had abandoned my papers and red pen. I clutched my purse and book-bag and ran to the curb where I bent over and threw up. I vomited until I thought I had vomited my stomach lining. I didn't know what to do or where to go. I was living in Martil, alone. I was teaching in the university, alone. And I was retching in the street, alone.

My watch showed that I had half-an-hour to get to my class so I wiped my mouth, found a mentholated throat lozenge and walked to the corner. I took a taxi back to the campus and gave the driver a dollar for a thirty-five cent ride. I did not want to have any exchange with anyone and I didn't want to touch his hand.

I went to class because I did not know where else to go. There were no options. I had to go to the university. At least I was safe because there was nothing else that could affect the numb person I called me. My walk back into the grammar class was automatic and with energy that came from some unknown place in my body.

The grammar class was smaller than usual and I did not have to yell as loudly as I usually do. Perhaps attendance was low because it was so hot and everyone smelled, especially me. While I apathetically delivered a monologue to the students where I explained in amazing detail the difference between

---

* Yosef Avrahami and Vadim Norzhich mistakenly entered Palestinian controlled Ramallah where they were brought to police headquarters. A violent mob of Palestinians stormed the building and tortured the soldiers to death, mutilating and defiling their bodies beyond recognition.

"feel bad" and "feel badly," a girl got up, crossed in front of me, and walked out. I had noticed Jenet before today because she was beautiful and was one of the few students who wore makeup, dressed in western style clothing and had her jet-black hair cut in a Farah Fawcett/Charlie's Angels style. Today, she had on a pale blue t-shirt with matching pants and black platform sandals. I noticed that she had a flat little toe with a triangular toenail. She looked like she was from Miami. A few minutes later two of her friends got up, crossed in front of me, and left the class. This was unusual. Two more students got up, so I decided that I had better see what the attraction was. I told the whole class to write two sentences using "feel bad" in one sentence and "feel badly" in the other.

The vision of the girls baked into clay statues on the hot pavement startled me. Gathered around Jenet, they energetically poured water down her throat. When I approached, all but two moved away. Jenet's eyes were rolled back in her head and she shook like crazy. This seizure was just five feet away from me. I watched the girls continue to flood her lungs with water.

Then I yelled, "Stop that! Don't pour water down her throat! She'll drown!"

"She's sick."

"She's having a fit."

"Look at her!" they replied hysterically in unison.

Clueless and inexperienced at medical emergency management, I said, "Put cold water on her head and hold her."

I went back to the class and talked about the sentences but the girls were still out there. I gave another five-minute exercise and went outside. There was no school protocol on how to handle emergencies. My room was ten minutes from the department office that had no telephone. I was in a haze or some kind of robotic trance because I didn't know what to do or where to go for help. My numb brain could not make any practical decisions.

At my request, they had changed their routine. The water went on her head and orange juice down her throat. I knew that she would die during my class and I did not have the energy to deal with this. Her T-shirt had huge wet spots that showed her bra and the roundness of her breasts. Her sopping hair was lying flat against her twitching head and her lips had no color. I thought I saw her stop breathing. She made jerky movements that were somewhat different, definitely diminished, compared to the ones a few minutes ago. Suddenly, she calmed down, the twitches waned, and the whites of her eyes changed to eyeballs with irises and pupils and tired life. I assigned two girls to stay outside with her and shooed the others back into the class. She lay across the laps of the two robed girls and she floated, just as the Israeli soldier had floated. I blinked to keep my vision clear because I didn't know what I was seeing anymore. My eyes were open but comprehension was impossible.

I stood in front of the class and knew that I could not go on. I had been drained of every ounce of energy that I had. I was scared. I was worried. I was depressed. I was ready to pack up. I dismissed the class early, went outside to find that the girls were gone. I didn't care. I didn't know who took Jenet's books and purse but there was no one left in the room and it didn't matter. I switched off the lights, turned around and phlegmatically walked out.

If I had had a ticket to go home that day, I would have gone right to the airport. Instead, I found myself in the back seat of a hot taxi. This time there was only one other passenger who solemnly sat in the front seat. I spread out my purse and book-bag and began to seriously attack my chalk dust-encrusted fingernails. First, I stripped the dried cuticles from my left thumb, then my index finger and finally my long finger started to bleed. I don't know if this was self-mutilation or an examination to see if I still had blood, but it was dogged determination. I looked at my bleeding finger and saw the

Palestinian's bloody hands. Suddenly, I thought of Christ's hands, his blood, the nails pounded into his flesh, my bloody finger. I thought, "I'm going to die right here, on this spot, right here in this taxi on Miramar Street and every year there will be a pilgrimage to this site where my blood will make lame people walk, blind people see, and barren women pregnant." Now I was sure this was an hallucination and all I had had was the cough drop!

Somehow, I got home though I don't remember the journey. At four o'clock that hot October day, I crawled into bed and lay there, like a corpse, beneath the two opaque glass windows in the bedroom. My red shoes were on the floor next to the bed and my clothes were still on. I had not washed my face. I had not put the night retainer on my perfectly straight teeth. I had not taken my calcium. I had not dispatched my daily e-mail. The best I could do was inhale and then exhale, which I did for fourteen hours without the slightest movement. The light stayed on all night and nothing moved in this house in Martil. It was as if the world had stopped.

BLACK BAG

My adjustment process continued. Not every minute was difficult and some were actually pleasant and fun. One aspect of this early time in Morocco was that I reacted to events quite differently than I did at home. I surprised myself with quick decisions, calmness, inappropriate reactions and a variety of other behaviors. I worried about losing things and about the chance of an encounter with a pickpocket or a scam artist. It was ironic that when my husband came, his pocket was picked numerous times and many, though not all attempts to snitch his money were foiled. However, when I was alone, this was a constant worry.

The routine of my day was not so different from my colleagues, since most of us in Martil used taxis and buses to get everywhere because teachers, even university professors, cannot afford cars. I liked to walk in areas where there were businesses because I got a feel for the country and its people. The Moroccan on the street was not interested in strangers or in any niceties related to strangers. If I were bumped or if I bumped someone, there was neither an apology exchanged nor even a hesitation. This was in contrast to the private Moroccan who would give you anything and do anything to make a visitor happy. An example was when I had tea at the home of my department chair's aunt.

"What is that on the handle of the teapot?" I asked.

"This?" she answered.

"That little white thing."

She held up a little white cotton bird. "The handle burns my hand. Here." She insisted that I take it.

"No, I couldn't."

With that she put it in my purse.

When I ate couscous at a student's house and asked about the difference between couscous and tagine, the mother brought out a huge tagine pot and said, *"Henayah"* (here) and when I said, *"La, la. Shokrun."* (No, No. Thank you,) she was insulted that I did not take it home with me.

The taxi situation was another challenge. Ismael once quipped, "Morocco is Mercedes Hell," because all the old Mercedes from Europe were sent here and these tubercular taxis were thirty-year-old diesels that had been forced back into full-time service. I loved looking at this country through his eyes because, in spite of its faults, he loved Morocco and also admired the taxi system. The taxis would not begin their morning route until there were four passengers in the back seat and two in the passenger seat. In the beginning, I rented the whole front seat and paid two fares but since all of the taxis had non-functioning seat belts, sported fractured windshield glass on the passenger side, and were driven at speeds faster than sound, I determined that the back seat was safer and decided to pay four dirhams (total one dollar) in order to enjoy the entire rear seat solo. The mystery of the spiritual world of old Mercedes did not encourage me to go to my own Paradise, so I tried to find the safest and most expedient way to get around. However, I began to feel guilty when I realized that Moroccans had to wait for another taxi when I rented so many seats. During early morning hours this could be a fifteen-minute wait. Finally, I decided that I would squeeze into the back seat every morning with the other passengers.

One hot, sticky morning, I was jammed into the back seat between three men. The one on my right leaned into my thigh and the one on my left was perched on my hip. I positioned myself so I could clutch my black nylon purse under my green book-pack and look directly ahead at the back of a man's hairy neck and straight black hair. I crowded people with my bags but didn't care since early in my stay I decided never to put anything in the trunk because I was afraid I would forget about it. Both men in the right front seat had different shades of gray shirts on and the three men in back were also neutral in their dress; however, the four of us in the back seat had on sandals though mine were red. I felt like a flower against this neutral backdrop.

As this joy ride commenced in my furnace on wheels, I looked to my right and a man with no front teeth was clutching my purse in his lap. I said in perfect English, "You will be singing soprano if you don't give me my purse," which, of course, he didn't do since he did not understand what I was saying. This little warning was my mantra whenever a stranger approached me and it gave me courage when I might have chosen to run or scream; however, in this hot intimate encounter, it proved useless. Again, I demanded my purse. Still, he did not understand me. I pointed to my black bag and went after it. He retracted his whole body and leaned into the unsuspecting, unshaven fellow next to him who gasped while the culprit cradled my bag. I tried to yank the purse from him and he pulled it again and I pulled and he pulled.

"Ha!" I yelled with my Japanese Samurai voice, and still he held on to the purse.

Finally, my adrenaline kicked in so I shouted, "You son of a bitch," and pulled my bag from him. Our fellow passengers in front did not have room to turn around to witness my victory, but the spectators next to us gave a running commentary to the excluded driver. My victim did not look very happy but I was brazenly triumphant.

The prize was in my left hand so I moved my green book-pack to return the black bag to its proper place and there, in my lap, under my book-bag, sitting exactly where I had wedged it ten minutes earlier, was my black nylon purse. My puzzled compatriot sweated profusely while I was planted in a puddle of sticky cotton because it felt like my skirt had liquefied. I figured that I had three options: (1) Jump out of the speeding taxi but I couldn't do that because this one had no door handles and the driver held some kind of a tool that he would lend you when you needed to exit. (2) Give him money but I couldn't do that because I was afraid to open my wallet in public. (3) Tell him how much I love his purse and ask him where I could buy one for my husband. So in my pitiful French, I sputtered, "*Monsieur, j'adore votre sac. Où achete vous le sac parce que je voudrais le meme sac pour mon marier?*" However, he spoke no French and looked at me as if I were crazy, so I just stroked his purse, returned it to his lap, and then allowed him to return to his previous position on my thigh.

When I saw the sanctuary of the university, I said, "*Henayah,*" and the driver slammed on the brakes, gave the precious tool to the unshaven man with the little white skullcap, at the right rear door, took my money and watched me exit. I never turned around but just stood up as tall as five-feet-three-inches could, hefted the green backpack on my back, put the accursed black purse in my right hand and strutted to my first class.

The first class on this day was the grammar class, which was the hardest class for me to teach. The class averaged eighty-five students a day and was taught in a long narrow room where students shared desks and crowded together on benches. At the end of class, I was unable to speak because I had to yell to be heard.

Ismael said, "Get a microphone from the administration."

"Where is it? Which room?"

"The offices don't have numbers."

"How do I know where to go?"

"Gloria, ask for administration."

With those instructions, it took an hour to find the right secretary.

"Hi! I'm Gloria and I teach freshman English in Room F12. There are over eighty students. Do you think I could have a microphone?"

"F12?" She opened her book, looked up and shook her head. "*La, la.* Sorry, no electric plugs in that room."

"*Shokrun.*" I smiled. "*Shokrun et salaam.* See you later."

The students squeezed together in the front seats and half of the girls wore headscarves that must have raised their body temperature ten degrees. The classroom did not smell fresh.

The students expected me to dictate rules of grammar rather than lecture or give interactive exercises. When I tried the American way of teaching grammar, the students kept interrupting me. "Gloria, what's the rule?" Ibraheem queried with a big smile.

"Let's figure out the rule," I smiled.

"That's not how we do it here."

"I know," I smiled again.

Finally, Ibraheem, who was the class spokesman, said, "Gloria, we can't afford to buy the books. They're too expensive. You *must* dictate the rules to us or we'll flunk."

Jenet, who sat in the second row, raised her hand and looked so pathetic, I felt compelled to call on her. "Gloria, all of the freshman classes take the English final together. If you don't give us the rules, the other classes will have rules we don't know."

"That's ridiculous. You want me to stand up here everyday and dictate pages out of a rule book."

Absolute silence.

"I don't believe you," I said and suddenly, I believed them.

It was a tedious, arduous process but I did what they expected because all of the instructors taught like this.

A few days later I caught Drissa, the department chair. "Drissa, the freshman English class said they can't afford to buy the books that the university requires of the class."

She looked at me. "That's right."

"Am I supposed to just stand up in front of the class and dictate the rules?"

"I don't know how you're going to do it. You're the teacher. How's the apartment going?"

"Drissa, let's talk about the apartment later... They also said that about half the class will flunk the freshman year."

"No, it's closer to 80 percent."

"How do you know it'll be 80 percent?"

"It's automatic and necessary since there's no entrance exam. We don't have the resources to educate the number of students who want to come here so we allow everyone who wants to go to the university to attend for one year. Then we select the top 20 percent, no matter what the grades are, and we flunk the rest." She walked away. With a toss of her hair, she had dismissed any more questions I might have had.

I later learned that they literally do what Drissa described. They draw a line at the 20-percent mark beginning with the student who has the highest grades. At the 20-percent mark, they cut the class. This is regardless of the score of the next student even if he or she is tied with the one above the 20-percent mark. I never found out what they did if the line divided a few students with the same grades. The cruelty of this class selection process distressed me. It was through these eyes that I viewed this class and the stress with which the students lived.

I now know why the students like to hear me as I stand in front of class and relate the adventures of Gloria. I am probably one of the few instructors who shares her human side. They laugh at my funny stories when I describe whatever has happened to me in my everyday life. This monologue turns into a show the first five minutes of class each day but this "black bag day" has me in no mood to entertain. I am weak, wet, and sapped of all my energy; and it is just eight in the morning.

At ten o'clock I welcome the four-hour break between classes and taxi back to my house in Martil. It is always so quiet here that after lunch I habitually fall asleep, sitting straight up, on the couch and wake up shocked that I have only a half-hour to get back to school.

However this day is different. I grab my backpack full of books, my black bag and my keys, and go to open the front door. The key slides in the lock but the bolt will not turn. I kick the iron door. I push. I pull. There is no reaction. I push so hard that the key cuts my index finger. I bleed all over the place. I quickly put on a Band-Aid from my medicine bag and go back to the door, repeat these futile actions with no success. Then I decide to jump out the window. I run to the front salon, pull back the flowered curtains, open the window only to see that there are bars on the windows. I try to open them from the inside but they are locked with huge, rusted padlocks. I call Jamel, whom I continually curse because of his insistence that I rent this house when I wanted to live in an apartment in Tanger.

"Hi! It's Gloria. I have a *mushkila*."

"What is it this time?" His impatience is obvious.

"Sorry to bother you. I am locked in."

"You're locked out?"

"No. I'm locked in. I can't get the key to turn the bolt from the inside. Remember, we had trouble with it the first day."

"I showed you how to do it."

"I watched you but I'm still locked in. I have a class in twenty-five minutes. Please come."

"I'll be right over."

"*Shokrun*"

He literally lives five minutes from my prison. I stand at the window and watch for him through my cell bars while I squint into the blaring sun. It takes him over an hour to get to my house. I throw the keys out the window, lock the window, and meet him at the door. He is annoyed.

"Why can't you figure out how to open this door?"

I don't answer him. I just think about what I would like to do with the iron door.

My afternoon class, a literature class, has patiently waited for me. They do not appear to have been inconvenienced at all. They are a wonderful class and for me, to have these nineteen students plus William Shakespeare for two hours is a blessing. We are studying *Romeo and Juliet.* Laila reads Juliet's lines. I observe this beautiful twenty-year-old woman dressed in a long light green robe with a flowered headscarf that covers all of her head plus half of her forehead. I remember when I realized, "This is the miracle I wished for. I have connected with the students and together; we have found and loved Shakespeare." Laila is actually very good and when she reads the lines,

> "Give me my Romeo, and when I shall die
> Take him and cut him out in little stars
> And he will make the face of heaven so fine
> That all the world will be in love with night,
> And pay no worship to the garish sun."

I cry for Juliet and for myself.

Her Romeo, Khalid, is a small boy with thick glasses and very big teeth. When he reads Romeo, he is a tall handsome Italian prince. I applaud and yell, "Bravo!"

They bow and I cannot imagine being more moved.

Khalid asks me to join them after class for an assembly in the courtyard, so I put on my backpack, grab my purse and go to the main quadrangle where hundreds of students are assembled. There are songs, cheers and a kind of step-march in place because there really is nowhere for them to march to so they must walk in place in this small open quadrangle. I hoot and clap and really get into this homecoming type exercise. I love everyone here.

Finally I ask, "Say, what's the song? Great beat."

"Oh, we're protesting against the Jews because of the war in Palestine," Khalid answers with a look as if he expects me to agree and to understand.

"The Intifada?" I am frightened and again remember how terrified I was in Fes. Here, there is no Israel, so I ask, "The Intifada in Palestine?"

"The war against the Jews."

Again, I feel I am about to vomit out of fear. My insides start to shake. I must have looked green because Laila yelled, "Gloria, what's wrong?"

For some reason, maybe in an effort not to belie the terrible emotional upheaval I had just experienced, I speak about a headache, *"J'ai mal a la tête."*

Laila grabs my backpack and she, Khalid and a few of the other students help me wend my way through the enthusiastic crowd out to the hot street where they hail a taxi for me. Again, I plant myself in a pool of sweat in the crowded back seat of the taxi. I need to get to a cyber café for my dose of America. I need my e-mail. My favorite Internet café is about six blocks from my house. I walk there baked by the merciless sun and find the door rolled up. This little windowless café looks like a one-car garage and actually has a garage door as the front. The walls are white and the floor is gray concrete. Even though it is a café, there is no food, no waiter, and no aromatic spice smells. It has six computers plus one copy machine lined up against the walls. I go here for two reasons. The first is that it is the only one in town that has the software to change the keyboard to perform like an American keyboard so that when I hit the first key with the little finger of my left hand, I get 'a' and not 'q.' The second reason is that I adore Hassan, the manager. He is about thirty, tall, thin, bearded and with fabulous teeth. Everyday when I come in, I pat the top of his head while he works at the computer and without turning, he smiles and says "Hi Gloria!" He always sounds happy to see me.

However, today there is no Hassan. He is in Tanger for the day. I sit at my computer waiting for the assistant to turn my computer on. He keys in the password three times but nothing happens. Only Hassan knows all the passwords and he isn't here. I can't send or receive any e-mail today. I've lost my only connection to the outside world, to my family, my friends, my reality, my beautiful America.

Suddenly, I am aware of the birds that flock to the tree at the door of the café at sundown. They screech and shake the whole tree. I hear them at the same time I hear myself crying. The assistant yells something at me in Arabic but it doesn't stop my crying. I smile through my tears and yell, "*Shokrun.*" There is no way to explain to him or even use hand signals that will describe how and why I am upset. I wipe my hot, wet face and walk home.

I look at my house as I approach it and realize that it has always had bars but I, oblivious to so much, had never noticed them. I chastise myself for being so terrified at night. Obviously, no one can get in because, as I well know, no one can get out. But, I am not reassured. I put the key in the lock. Nothing happens. I have little strength in my hand because when I put pressure on the key, my finger starts to bleed. There are no neighbors and if there were, how would I communicate with them? Luckily, I had keyed the owner's name into my cell phone. I call Mo, my non-English speaking landlord, and I think he says he will be right over. It is almost dark and the streetlight goes on, so I feel better. However, an hour and a half later, all of the mosquitoes in North Africa and I are sitting on the front step waiting for Mo. He drives up waving, opens the front door, and starts to leave, but I signal for him to stand there and hold the door open. I run to get a roll of strapping tape that I use to tape the offending lock in place so that it is out of play with the rest of the door. There is still one remaining deadbolt that I can lock, plus an interior slide lock. I feel secure.

"Thank you Mo. *Shokrun.*" I smile as he mutters something in Arabic. My hassled landlord can't wait to leave while his hassled tenant can't wait to lock the door and end the day.

I am drained but for some reason not depressed. Or, at least, I don't think I am depressed. I try to figure out how I feel. It isn't that I am so lonely but I am really alone. I know that if I lock the door to my house and fall down the steps, break my leg, no one will miss me for two weeks. My husband will not know where to call. The house has no phone. My cell phone works only half the time. What am I feeling? Confusion? Yes. Faceless and nameless? Yes. I try to think of the good things about today. I did love the Shakespeare class. I loved Laila crying. I adored our Romeo. I thought my purse had been stolen and even though I was mistaken, I had the strength to go after it, to watch out for myself, even if I had acted like a lunatic. It is just that each step is so hard. I want to coast a little and yet, when I try, I get lost. I know intellectually that this is all part of the adjustment process. Sometimes when I look in the mirror at my sixty-two-year-old face, I see a blank look that disturbs me. It is hard adapting to another culture. Each day is difficult but I have to remember that each day has its successes too. Even this day. I don't know if I believe that myself. But I keep repeating it anyway.

FATIMA AND ABDELHAI

This was my second to last night in Martil before moving to the luxurious apartment in Tanger. I was leaving the resort town of white stucco buildings, white sand, aquamarine sea and empty houses. This night was spent with the only friends that I had there, Fatima and Abdelhai. They too were stuck in a different part of this ghost town. We met every day and laughed and tried to decide who was more miserable.

"Fatima, you aren't more miserable because there is a cat that spends the winter near you." A big tear rolled over her long lower lashes but only in her left eye. Then I knew she was more miserable. She struggled with 'forever' while my struggle was with 'temporary.'

We laughed about the way we met which was in a cyber café that had no functioning Internet that day. Two women, sitting in a dark room surrounded by twenty computer screens that were blank, nowhere to go and nothing to do but wait for the power or the connection to *Yahoo*. Fatima said she spoke first but I knew that I had because I always asked everyone, "Do you speak English?" Most people looked blank. However, this day, I struck gold. There she was sitting with her thick glasses, long curly hair, no make-up, jeans, tennis shoes, and huge brown eyes. I decided she might speak English, so I said, "Speak English?"

Fatima said, "Not good."

"I can't believe it!"

"I don't speak English a lot."

"I don't care if all you know is the alphabet. Will you be my friend?"

We chatted for two hours that Saturday afternoon. The power never was turned on but it didn't matter. I had made human contact. In fact, she asked me to join Abdelhai, her husband, and her the following Sunday morning at 10:30 in front of their favorite cyber café.

That Sunday morning I woke at six. I started to get dressed immediately as if this were my first date, though there was absolutely nothing to do for the next four hours because everything was closed. The hours crawled but at ten I was waiting for Hassan to roll up the door. He was only fifteen minutes late. I sat down and quickly dispatched the disk I had filled last night with cheerful e-mails to everyone. Meanwhile, Hassan and his assistant were cleaning the copy machine. They were as involved as I was when suddenly there was a shriek in Arabic that meant nothing to me. Simultaneously, a black cloud mushroomed around me; a floating, hovering cloud. Small black particles engulfed me. I sat there dumbfounded and heard a clink on the back of my folding chair, a crash on the floor, and some loud Arabic words. Literally, the dust settled and there I was, surrounded by the ink from the cartridge that one of the men had dropped en route to the garbage can but was intercepted by the back of my chair. I didn't move. Hassan didn't move. His assistant didn't move. Maybe, it was only ten seconds of a frozen time frame where nothing moved. Then I turned and looked at two horror-stricken faces that were looking at someone who looked as if she had just jumped out of a coal chute.

Luckily Hassan thought quickly. It was obvious why he was the manager. He had two cotton balls on the desk that he used to clean something on the computers and he started dabbing at my pants leg as if to clean the dry ink off. There were two problems. He could not touch me because he was Muslim and he had nothing to offer me anyhow. I was covered in dry ink. His assistant was speaking very quickly in Arabic. I had no idea what he was saying.

Hassan said, "Gloria, I don't know what to do."

"Let me think about it."

"Do you think you should move?"

"Hassan, where should I go if I move?" There was no bathroom in this garage.

"Let me think about that."

"What do I look like?"

"A Senegalese."

"Black?"

"Very black."

"Do you have a paper towel?"

"I'll send Ahmed to the grocery."

Within two minutes, panting and sweating, Ahmed returned to the café with three purse-size packages of tissues that he ripped open and put on my computer. Gently and carefully, I dabbed around my eyes and mouth. I stood up and looked at my arms and khaki pants. They were dusted as was the dark brown Land's End zippered sweatshirt that I immediately removed. I jumped up and down about seven or eight times and, as stupid as it may have looked, some of the ink floated off me. Ahmed brought two glasses of water from the grocery and with the tissues and water, I prepared for my date with Fatima and Abdelhai. My khakis were filthy but my T-shirt had been saved because the sweatshirt had been draped over my shoulders. Fatima, Abdelhai and I laughed all day about our first Sunday together. In spite of this unpropitious first encounter, we spent every Sunday together.

Abdelhai was a landscape architect who had studied at Versailles for four years. He was brilliant and creative. Fatima had a university degree also, but I never understood what it was in. She was fluent in Classical and Moroccan Arabic, English, French, and Spanish. She was a French translator but because her mother was from Seville, Spanish was her first language. Both were twenty-nine years old. Abdelhai managed and landscaped the grounds of the Cabo Sur Country Club and Resort. Part of his stipend was a free apartment overlooking the Mediterranean Sea. The only problem was that either the entire resort was empty during the off-season or it was over-filled beyond capacity during the summer season. Neither time was conducive to good living, yet the price was right. They too lived in an abandoned part of town.

They were trying to emigrate from Morocco to Montreal, as they knew they had no future in Morocco. They felt their country had no future in this world.

"I must escape," Fatima said. "My mother and brother went to Spain after my dad died in '95.'"

Abdelhai added, "I can't work there because landscape architecture is not a licensed profession. France is out because they don't want any more Moroccans."

"Abdelhai sent in our papers to go to Montreal so maybe we'll go there."

They had made the first cut and had filed a second set of papers for the immigration process. It was tedious, lengthy, something that plagued them each day, and also made them anxious about their lives. There was always a sadness surrounding Abdelhai because he didn't want to leave either his family or his country, yet Fatima never stopped pushing. She hated the thought of the rest of her life being wasted in Morocco. No one was here for her. Mentally, she had moved away when her mother left Morocco.

"This is a desert," she said.

"Abdelhai has a wonderful job here, Fatima, and you do too."

"We'll die here," she murmured.

"I work too hard. During the summer, I need three batteries a day on my mobile phone because I have no time to charge it. The club won't let me hire more help."

"I never see Abdelhai during the summer," she complained. "Besides he has returned to being a Muslim man. When he first returned from France, he touched me. Yesterday, when I was crossing the street with him, I grabbed his arm because a car came too close to me. He pushed me away—in the middle of the street. He's like all the rest."

I thought about how we teased him because he had lived with a French woman when he was a graduate student in Versailles. This was not the same man who could live openly with an unmarried woman

Abdelhai played with his cell phone and never looked up. Finally, he glanced at me and not at Fatima. I always looked straight into his black eyes that were huge but surprising because he wore some kind of non-reflective glass in his glasses which made it appear as if he were wearing frames without lenses. However, this time his eyes looked sad and small. He was not happy with Fatima's criticism.

"Gloria, I will die here. We must leave." She looked at her long nail-bitten fingers.

There was nothing more to say.

My week was now organized around time with Fatima. Weekdays, we went to different cyber cafés but at the same hour. I needed to go to Hassan's because he had an English keyboard, whereas Fatima felt my "garage café" was depressing. We met afterwards and chatted each evening. Sometimes they drove me home and sometimes I walked by myself in the beautiful twilight.

One evening, they returned to my house with me. I had left the TV on all day while I was gone so that I wouldn't walk into a dead house. The news was on and while I went to get some diet Cokes from the kitchen, Abdelhai sat down to watch. I heard him yell in French but I couldn't understand it. I ran to the TV salon where he was now standing in front of the TV screen watching the news while Fatima sat frozen on the couch watching Abdelhai's back. Abdelhai continued to yell in Arabic. I said, "What about me? *Je ne comprende pas.* I don't understand."

Abdelhai turned to me, agitated, blinking and stiff. "The fucking Jews bombed a Palestinian office which killed four Palestinians. Yesterday, two Jewish kids were killed. Now look what they've done." He began yelling in Arabic again. He blocked the screen with his body so I sat down next to Fatima. Her pale skin whitened. Silently, we both watched Abdelhai's back. While we waited for the newscast to end, Abdelhai turned off the TV. After a minute or two, he sat down and the three of us opened our drinks. I felt blank-faced and as hard and cool as the marble under my feet while the words "fucking Jews" resonated inside my hollow tear drained head.

I wouldn't react this time. I tried to remain quiet.

"It looks pretty bad over there." I finally broke the silence.

"It's hell for those poor people," he uttered. "Do you have a beer?"

"Sorry Abdelhai, I don't drink. Next time you come though, I'll have one for you." Most Muslims don't drink because liquor is forbidden but the foreign-educated have learned to enjoy drinking. This Abdelhai had not forgotten.

"I have some cheese, baguette and yogurt. Would you have a light dinner with me? It's meager but whatever I have, I'd love to share."

"No, we must go home now. See you tomorrow evening." Fatima leaned over to hug me while Abdelhai went to the door and waited for Fatima and me to finish our kissing ritual.

Impatiently he commanded, *"On y va Fatima!* Let's go." She ran to the front door and left. He turned and silently walked out.

I bolted the door and sat down in front of the TV. After this I knew I had to keep myself together and stay strong. I didn't cry. I didn't shake. I just sat. My only two friends in all of Martil had showed me exactly how they felt about the Intifada. I could no more say to them, "Hey guys! I just want you to know that I'm Jewish, but we shouldn't let that color our friendship!" I knew that I would have to eliminate that thought from my mind. I had to become a nothing, but how could I rid myself of these feelings, these fears, and these thoughts that never left my brain? I worried that I might speak Yiddish when I bumped my shin. I worried that I might refer to Dick as *Saba*, the Hebrew word for grandfather. I worried that I might look too Jewish. I worried.

I did not turn on the TV again that night. Instead, I read *The Red Tent* by Anita Diamant, polished my toenails bright red and put some e-mail on a disk to send at the cyber café the next day. I went to sleep about eleven o'clock and slept until three when I awoke with the realization that I was totally alone, a Jewish woman in an Arab country. I wondered what my original thoughts were that had led to choosing this place to live.

THE MAID AT THE HOUSE IN MARTIL

Two days after I had moved into the house at Martil, Jamel had asked Mo, the landlord, if he could find a maid for me. He was happy to do this and he said, "She'll be there Monday morning."

Monday morning the doorbell rang and a young woman in a tan *jallabah*, brown scarf, and black purse was standing at my door. I motioned for her to come in and she entered and took off her scarf and robe. It was about one hundred degrees and I could smell sweat when she took off these warm outer garments. She understood neither my French nor my Arabic. We toured every room upstairs and downstairs. The first thing she did was to pick up the dirty clothesbasket and carry the clothes outside to a sink in the back yard. There she soaked the clothes in a plastic pan of cold soapy water, washed them on the cement sink's scrub board, and hung them on the clothesline. Then she went in the house to begin her cleaning regimen. Her long brown hair was tied in a long knot and she wore no lipstick. She was a petite woman who wore a dress and bedroom slippers as her uniform. She removed the slippers when she washed the floors on her hands and knees.

I gave her an extra key to the house and when she was finished, she kissed me on both cheeks, rubbed my cheek with a sandpaper hand, and said something in Arabic. I responded, "*Smee* Gloria," which I thought meant "I'm Gloria' but she didn't respond. I paid her and waved good-bye. My house was clean enough to function as an operating room.

This woman, whose name I never learned, came to my house three times a week for the four weeks I lived in Martil.

I called Jamel, "Please remind Mo that I'll be leaving at the end of October."

"Why?"

"We discussed this the day I signed the lease."

"Oh."

"Also, I don't know the maid's name. Can you ask Mo? And please, Jamel, she needs to know I'm moving."

"Sure. Good-bye."

"Bislammah Salaam."

He never called back.

One day I made a motion like a baby and the next day, the maid brought pictures of her baby. I gave her an extra five dollars for the baby that day but never did learn his/her name and still did not know hers.

The last day of work, she arrived to find all my suitcases and boxes lined up next to the front door. She looked at them. She looked at me.

I shook my head and said, "No Martil. Tanger."

"Mo?" I was trying to ask her if the landlord, Mo had told her.

She understood and shook her head no.

I said, *"Barak' allahu fik,"* which meant "Allah bless you" and is a sincere, deep felt way of expressing appreciation. It is a closing sentence.

She now understood that I was moving. Jamel and Mo never bothered to give her the message; to them it was of no importance. She sat down on the long blue couch in the upper salon. She slumped back; her legs spread into an inverted V. She sat for a moment and then started to sob. She had no job after that day and I had no way of communicating with her. I had tried to write words from my Arabic class but I realized she was illiterate. My attempts at drawing the face of a sad person were no help.

She sobbed and sobbed. I gave her eighteen dollars, three days' pay, kissed her cheeks and walked her to the door. She never turned around. I locked the door, got the broom and for the last time, swept the floor in my house in Martil.

MOVING TO TANGER

My last night in this house in Martil was one in which I did not sleep at all. I kept getting up, lying down, closing my eyes and then remembering another place where I might have put a treasured belonging. I would look in a cabinet, behind a door, on the clothesline, everywhere, but there was never anything because I had gone through this same ritual the night before and probably, the night before that. This crazy cycle continued all night. Sometimes I shook inside but I knew that would be better when I moved to Tanger. I hoped.

My belongings had multiplied because I had to buy an additional suitcase in the Medina where I bargained mercilessly to get it for two dollars and fifty cents. It resembled a plaid plastic shopping bag with a zipper. I saw a version of this bag attached to almost every Moroccan traveling on the buses or trains and it looked quite durable. So, with my five foot long duffel bag, which I could not move and which I had to pack while it was parked in the front hall, my huge red and yellow twenty-nine-inch Skyway suitcase, my carry-on Eiffel rollaboard, the plastic suitcase, green backpack, and three book boxes, I was ready to go.

A group of students volunteered to help me move. This presented a perfect opportunity to discuss the American concept of being on time that is completely foreign to them. I also gave them maps with a stick drawing of me standing in front of the bakery, *panederia* or *boulangerie*. At 9:45 I began the expected wait for our 10:00 A.M. *rendez-vous*. Before posting myself on the designated corner, I decided to thank the few working merchants who had been nice to me. When I said good-bye to these storekeepers and service people, I realized that the people I had met here were generally very helpful and appreciative of foreigners. Granted, they liked our money, as my friend Willie told me, but they were also flattered by our presence and our interest in their country. It is amazing how much you can convey with grunts and pictures. I carried around a little spiral notebook to draw pictures of things I wanted, such as scotch tape, candles, and the infamous batteries. It was a perpetual challenge.

By noon, six students had gathered on the corner.

Abune said, "Gloria, I think this is as big as the group is going to get."

Bahia agreed and said, "Drissa will be at the bus station when we get there, so seven people will be enough."

"We're used to carrying a lot on buses," the boys added in unison.

The two stick-thin boys, Abune and Brahim together carried the duffel bag suspended between them and the rest of us loaded our backs with the remaining baggage.

We walked very slowly to the taxi stand and then the fun began. We tried to fit the luggage into the boot of two taxis but there was just too much stuff. However, the taxi drivers were used to this, and the two drivers managed to pile all of the luggage in but were unable to close the trunks. Needless to say, no one had rope and I had never even thought of it, so with a shrug, the drivers told the students in Arabic that the luggage would be all right. Off we roared toward Tetouan with the trunk lids wide open, bouncing up and down on the pitted streets the entire half-hour. Amazingly, everything stayed exactly where it was supposed to.

The bus station is like no other place I have ever seen. There is no signboard displaying a schedule and I am not sure if this is because of the expense or because of the high illiteracy rate. Instead of signs, there are "yellers," men who walk around the bus station yelling the destination of his company's next bus. There are at least ten different bus companies; one company may have owned only one bus or like the state-run CTM that owned hundreds. Each company has a little five-by-five office with a ticket seller at a counter, a picture of the king, and a picture of the company's bus so that the illiterates, like me, can identify the red and blue wavy striped bus or the yellow bus. Above the door to some of the offices may be a handwritten or small printed Arabic sign with the schedule or some offices may have the departure times on the glass door or some may have absolutely nothing. However, the real communication is with each company's yeller. The names yelled have to be loud enough for passengers to hear so one yeller constantly bellows louder than the other companies' yeller. In addition to the yellers, there are people who then try to guide you to your bus and wait for you to give them money. They yell too. If you don't give them money, they follow you on to the bus, stand and wait until you reward them for showing you which bus to take. In addition to this noise, the perpetual sound of a TV blasts at full volume. On days when the soccer game is on, there are at least thirty men cheering and yelling with each play.

En route to the buses, which are parked in unmarked stalls in the bowels of the station, there are hawkers. These people shout the price of whatever they are selling. I have watched people buy necklaces, shampoo, food, candy, shoes, radios, batteries, live chickens and everything else that is portable. It is a real business center and it is noisy with mercantilism at its most animated level.

We managed to get the luggage loaded, tickets bought, and some chocolate for the bus. We had an hour-and-a-half ride and sitting on a quiet bus was a welcome relief. My only concern was that I had told Ismael, whose brother Adnane owned the flat, that we would be in Tanger by eleven and we were going to be three hours late.

I turned to the boy sitting next to me and said, "I'm so worried about making Ismael wait."

"Don't worry. We don't get upset about time."

"Thanks but I do. By the way, I saw the King's palace Wednesday. I peeked through the gate."

"Why'd you do that?"

"What? Peek through the gate?"

"Why did you go to the palace?"

"Oh, I guess because part of me is a tourist."

"Why the palace?"

I didn't answer because I wasn't sure where this was going.

"How can you even look at how he lives when the rest of us live so miserably?"

Again, I sat mutely because the conversation was blasphemous and I was frightened, so I smiled dumbly and looked at the rolling golden hills of northern Morocco.

When we arrived at the Tanger bus station, we called Ismael and he gave the address to the taxi drivers. The convoy of three *petit* taxis pulled into the parking area of the apartment to find Ismael and Elizabeth standing outside with big smiles. He told the kids to go up to apartment 7B while he and I went to the underground garage to get two more boxes. We then took the Otis elevator up to my beautiful new apartment and a new life! What a gem it was! Was I lucky!

We were starved for lunch. Immediately, we all left together, and Ismael wished me good luck while warning me not to be out after dark. He and Elizabeth had to pick up their son, Aziz, from a soccer game, so the kids and I were on our own.

Walking through Tanger was so exhilarating after having lived in Martil. There were crowds of all kinds of people on the street, crazy traffic, policemen, taxis, tourists, kids, and beggars. There was life! It was a sweet autumnal beginning. I think I smiled so long and hard that my jaw muscles hurt. I wanted to say "Thank you for being here," to each and every person I saw because I had been so alone and isolated in the ghost town.

The kids were thrilled to have a day in Tanger. We had pizza and cokes at an authentic Italian pizzeria. Afterwards, we went to the Medina. I told them that I needed a blanket and we walked around to get an idea of the prices. Then they made me go away while they bargained for a blanket. They were so excited that they were able to get a blanket for two dollars less than I had. Drissa, the tallest girl, wanted to call her mother immediately because it was the first time she had done this and it was a real accomplishment. She had been the lead negotiator. I also got some pillows and suddenly noticed that it was getting dark. Unfortunately, the day had to end.

I gave the kids bus money to get back to Tetouan and Martil, kissed all of them a dozen times, and then got into a taxi while they gave directions in Arabic to the driver as to where I lived and told me exactly how much to pay him. "Not a dirham more Gloria," warned Drissa with the tone of a mother's voice scolding her two-year old.

The driver drove right by the apartments and I had to yell at him to stop, but he didn't understand my English or French. Finally, when I retrieved the word for here, "*Henayah!*" he showed some recognition of my poorly pronounced Arabic. Making an immediate illegal U-turn, he deposited me in front of my apartment complex of three identical ten-story buildings.

Ismael and I had entered and exited my flat this afternoon and all other times from the unlighted parking garage under the building and now that it was dark I was not going down there alone. I couldn't believe that I didn't know which building I lived in. There were no numbers, no addresses, and no distinctive difference. The bells were lined up next to the entrance with the occupants' names clearly written in Arabic. The buildings were in a U-arrangement and were identical. I assumed that I had a one-in-three chance of going into the right building. I put my key in the entry door lock and, sure enough, it slid right in! However, it would not turn. I pushed and

~ 82 ~

pushed just as I had in Martil and the same spot on my right index finger started to bleed. Then I tried to pull the key out but it would not move. There I was standing with three pillows and a huge blanket in large plastic bags, looking at my key that now seemed to be permanently implanted in a door.

Finally, I saw a young couple walking by. She had on a light tan *jallabah* and black headscarf while he had on jeans, T-shirt and sandals. I waved to them, walked towards them and cried, "Help!" I don't think they understood the word but these non-English speakers did get the message. He ran up the steps. I pointed and he yanked the key out of the lock.

I thanked him profusely in Arabic and told him that I wanted Allah to bless him. He made motions to help me get in the right building but I shook my head and said, "No, no. I can do it. Okay. *Merci. Shokrun.*"

As he stood there, I waved vigorously to his wife or girlfriend and to him and started to go around to the next building. But I didn't realize that I was at the end of the property. I just walked backwards to the right of the building, facing the couple, smiling, constantly waving my hand, while holding the three pillows and blanket. Suddenly, I backed off the concrete porch down into a deep gully. My natural reaction was to scream but when I fell, I landed on the blanket and pillows and did not hurt myself. However, this couple did not know that. I looked up and saw two faces yelling down to me in Arabic and I started to laugh. The picture of me sprawled down this deep hole on top of a huge blanket and three pillows laughing like crazy only made me laugh more hysterically.

They were probably yelling, "Crazy lady, are you dead?"

Finally I was able to shout, "*Shokrun, bislammah, salaam.*" I waved good-bye and finally they shrugged their shoulders and stopped yelling to me. They left probably quite confused.

I managed to crawl up the embankment, eventually found my apartment, and locked myself in. I was disheveled, filthy, with cuts on my hands and right cheek, and probably would be stiff the next day. I couldn't believe what was continually happening to me, but like the indefatigable Eveready bunny, I kept going.

When I finally stopped and took a breath on this momentous night, I saw that the flat was a beautiful retreat that had the most amazing view of Spain, the Mediterranean, the Rock of Gibraltar and the mountains. The boardwalk had lights and I watched people stroll along the beach. The sky had deepened to a slate blue and the water was absolutely black this time of evening when it was nearly dark. There was a stream of cars making a necklace of lights along the divided street in front of the beach, and in the center parkway, spotlights illuminated huge palm trees. I thought, "I am living in a postcard." I kissed this day good-bye and went to sleep.

I slept so well the first night that I thought I must be dead. The mattress was wonderful and the bedroom was dark because I had left the metal shutters closed and there wasn't a sound. I couldn't believe how serenely happy I felt and that I was actually smiling even before getting out of bed. Just knowing that I was not in Martil was a joy.

I hurried to the front salon to take in the sea, Spain, Gibraltar, and the activity already in progress at seven in the morning. It was unreal. Ismael told me that artists say Morocco has some kind of hyper-illumination that means the light is different here. I don't know if they said this because of the blinding reflection of the light sand or the glittering of the blue sea. Whatever it was, it was breathtaking and it hurt my naked eyes. The bouncing light, the waves, and the movement of the sea hypnotized me. Tanger is hilly and in West Tanger I could see the Medina with its steep labyrinth of streets. There were hundreds of white egrets feeding in front of me among a flock of black-faced sheep. I felt as if this were heaven. I unpacked everything and found my binoculars because I didn't want to miss a thing.

My first outing was to go to the bus station where I was determined to figure out how to get to Tetouan by eight on Tuesday morning. It took about twenty minutes to walk there. It was a lot quieter at nine on a Sunday morning than it was yesterday afternoon. However, the yellers were still yelling and my job was to decipher the schedule.

I walked up to the most western looking of the yellers and ask, "Do you speak English?"

"Yes, I speak English and French and Arabic and Spanish and German and Hebrew."

"Why would a young Moroccan man like you speak Hebrew?" I innocently ask.

"I'm Jewish," he says so quietly that it sounds like he said, "I'm juice."

I pretend not to understand, "You're what?"

"Jewish, Sephardite, like Israel."

"Me too," I whisper into his ear.

"I can smell 'em," he says while wrinkling his nose. "Let me take you for coffee."

He yells something to the man sitting at the ticket desk of his bus company and walks to the snack bar in the bus station. I follow this little guy who walks with a swagger as he struts along in a black leather jacket, Levis, white socks and loafers. He winks, shakes my hand and announces, "I'm Amin."

"I'm Gloria," and I touch my heart to show him how sincere I am.

He takes out a Marlboro cigarette but I say, "I'm allergic."

He says, "All Jews are allergic."

The story is typical. "I've got no job. My brother gives me two bucks a day if I call the cities for him."

"That's a job."

"I have no future. Am I going to be doing this when I am forty?"

"What else can you see yourself doing?"

He says nothing.

"My uncle in America sends me clothes. Look!" He shows me the label in his jacket and it says Dayton's. "My uncle just got married and his wife says he can't send me clothes anymore. She's a witch."

I stir my coffee, which tastes like pure coffee grounds.

"Don't tell anyone you're Jewish," he warns me.

"Not even my best friend? Why?"

"Just don't or you'll have a lot of trouble. You can't trust these Arabs."

"Why?"

No answer from this talkative companion.

"Listen to me, dear Gloria." He lowers his head and in a quiet voice asks, "When are we going to party?"

"Party? What do you mean?" I ask.

"You know, go to your place and have a party. We'll have fun."

"Amin, I don't party. Do you know how old I am?"

"I like older women. They don't ask questions and aren't silly like young girls. With young girls, after you party, you gotta call them the next day."

"How old are you, Amin?"

"Twenty-eight and I've got no tomorrows. Come on and party with me." He is pleading.

"Amin, my youngest daughter is thirty-one and single. When she comes in, we will have you for dinner. I'm sorry, Amin. I have a husband so I party with him."

He doesn't answer and knows I am brushing him off. Again he says, "Gloria, don't tell anyone you're Jewish. It's bad here. The Israeli Embassy closed and everyone has gone home. I've been trying to get to Israel for two years and now

I'll never get there." He sits and stares. He is missing two teeth. I watch his smooth naked pink gum.

I don't know what to say to him because he is as depressed as my Muslim students are. His one hope of leaving Morocco and going to Israel has been blown up by suicide bombers. He has no tomorrow while I am sitting with a ticket to America. I have to protect myself from catching his depression and hopelessness. I am all that I have right now and I have to remain strong and upbeat.

He finishes his coffee and I let him pay for my mine, though I don't know why. I paid for Jamel's every meal the first week of my Moroccan experience. I have paid for so many other things with my students and an occasional coffee date with people from the department, yet I don't know why I didn't pay for this poor young man's coffee.

I shake hands with Amin and slip him a dollar. "See you Tuesday, Amin."

He doesn't answer but stands there staring at me. I turn and walk out of the bus station. From outside, I peer through the dirty glass door to see that he is still there, immobile, sculpted sadness, staring with dark depressed eyes.

I never see him again. I look for him every time I take a bus. Each day, I scrutinize the faces of all the yellers expecting to see Amin, but I don't see him and I cannot remember which bus company his brother works for.

BEYOND FES

When my first Sunday in my new city ended, I could hardly wipe the smile from my face. I must have walked ten miles during my explorations of Tanger. My tourist friends had told me that this place was the pits, but to me it was Mecca. I couldn't remember being so happy.

Ismael called to check on me and was surprised by the tone of my voice.

"Gloria, were you singing?"

"No, I am just happy."

Each day there was a new story. One day, Ismael told me, "I was a poor Moroccan immigrant in England and no doctor wanted to be assigned the likes of me but I was having a problem with piles. So, I went to the doctor and told him that I had piles. The doctor sat down on the examining table next to me and said, 'Benbouhia, I have piles. The Queen of England has piles. The Prime Minister has piles. Douglas Fairbanks has piles. Now go home and be happy that you have such good company.' So I went home and my roommate asked me what the doctor prescribed. 'Well,' I said, 'he didn't exactly prescribe anything. He just told me the Queen has piles too.'"

Ismael also told me that there was a woman who had spent a year in America living directly under me and that I should go and introduce myself. I met Fetouma the day after I moved in. After having spent a solo month in Martil, I was anxious to meet my neighbors. About 2:30 P.M. the next afternoon, I watched the big door to apartment 6B open. A young barefoot woman in jeans and a cotton crew neck sweater answered the door. I thought I was in the Midwest. Her curly hair was uncombed. She had no makeup on, big glasses, *café au lait* skin, a brown mole above her upper lip and smallish brown eyes. Her warmth jumped out the door of her apartment and sucked me in. We sat in the formal salon, which was furnished like my grandmother's living room. There was a huge mahogany credenza, two matching love seats, a mahogany coffee table, crystal lamps, an oriental carpet and every knickknack and picture you would find in an American home.

Fetouma looked and sounded like a native English speaker. Even now, if I close my eyes and listen to her, I think she is from Coffeeville, Kansas. She showed me pictures from her year in Oregon where she was a high school exchange student. This was followed by her return to Morocco in 1990 and subsequent marriage. Then, her brother went to Washington and remained in the US. She went to football games, Disneyland, Yosemite, skiing, snorkeling, and did everything else a privileged normal American high school student would do. We laughed over silly mistakes she had made, and that now I was making, in a new culture. I met her adorable children, but her husband, a first cousin, was out playing golf. We finished our tea, kissed and I said, "Good-bye my new friend. See you tomorrow."

The next day when I was walking up the stairs, I met a woman in a lime green *jallabah,* with a solid green headscarf obscuring all her hair and a lot of her forehead. I nodded and started to pass her but my left arm was grabbed and I was spun around to hear that flat prairie accent say, "That's a nice way to treat a friend!"

"Fetouma! It's you!"

"Yeah Gloria, and that's you!"

"I'm sorry Fetouma. I was a million miles away." I kept looking at this face trying to find my new friend.

Fetouma and I saw each other almost every single day of the week and our lives became closely intertwined. A few times we were able to recreate our first meeting, but after Dick arrived our husbands were usually involved and then she was always in her Arab dress. The contrasts were interesting because there were times I either borrowed or returned a cup of sugar or an egg and her husband would greet me in the front hall wearing his red plaid flannel pajamas. But Fetouma always wore a headscarf when she came to the door.

She was a devout Muslim who prayed five times a day and during Ramadan she prayed many more times, sometimes as many as fifteen, commencing at four in the morning and ending at midnight. I was never sure whether this was when Ramadan was only in the winter with the long nights or if every Ramadan was celebrated that way. Every year her parents spent the month of Ramadan in Mecca, as she had four years before, and since that time she has worn the *jallabah* and scarf daily. I asked her what made her change from a secular life. She talked about being close to Allah in Mecca and how the words of the Koran rang true to her. I saw pictures of her beautiful mother who wore European designer clothes. I never could figure out what Fetouma learned that her mother hadn't.

Fetouma spoke five languages fluently and studied the Koran two days a week. She said, "I feel Allah in every part of my life. Even today his words apply to each modern life situation." She knew her country as well as I know my street. She even knew which store in town was the "Jew's store." I never commented when this was mentioned. Deception was my constant companion. I felt there was no other route. I wondered how my face looked when she said things that upset me, but I found no confusion in her face. My days with her were wonderful, my conversations probing and open, and my friendship rich and rewarding. We were, in spite of everything, best friends.

DRISSA MARSU

Drissa is one of the students who adopted me and, with her best friend Bahia, was one of the students who had helped me move from Martil to Tanger. She and Bahia are always hiding in corners of the school just to surprise me, wave and kiss my cheeks. Drissa is very tall. Most of her clothes hide her figure but once I saw her without the bulky black jacket that she wears, whether it is hot or cold, and discovered that she is actually voluptuous. She could be the result of very expensive plastic body sculpting surgery, except on her face. Sometime in Drissa's life, she was cut from the left side of her nose, across the bridge perpendicularly and then down the cheek. The surgeon who stitched it up did it neatly but he did not match the skin exactly, so I am always aware of this puzzle being assembled almost perfectly. Drissa is tan. She has tan skin, tan eyebrows, tan eyelashes, and light brown eyes. Since she wears no lipstick, her lips are also tan. She wears a black scarf tied and pinned tightly around her head covering almost all of her forehead. This neutral palette is invaded by a radiant smile that is always on her face. She has a melodic voice that is only slightly above a whisper.

Drissa is very bright. She is one of sixteen living children and is somewhere near the third or fourth from the youngest. She is one of the groups of students, including Bahia, who joined me every Saturday for a field trip. She is a deeply religious young woman who constantly asked about my religiosity, "What religion are you Gloria?"

"*Je suis croyante.* I worship the same God you do."

"Then you must convert to Islam," she beamed. "I love you and want you to go to Paradise. You know that only Muslims will be allowed in Paradise."

"I think all good people will end up in the same place."

"But Gloria, *only good Muslims* can go to Paradise."

"Maybe, if I am truly good all my life, there will be a tiny space available for one non-Muslim."

Drissa smiled. "I hope so," she whispered.

Drissa's nineteen-year-old sister, Fatima, was getting married. She invited me to both the henna party and the wedding. I was uncomfortable going but could never refuse any of the students' requests.

After the Thursday grammar class ended at 6 P.M., I was again in Martil and needed to go to the bus station in Tetouan. I called Bahia when I got on the bus because I always confirmed every meeting two or three times since, invariably, I wound up in the wrong city, wrong block, or arrived at the wrong time. We verified that we were meeting at the bus station. I asked an ex-student to tell me when to get off so I could take a short cut to the bus station. He refused to tell me but insisted on going with me. I didn't know his name and told him not to bother, but he followed me off the bus. This was another instance where a Moroccan thought nothing of waiting and giving up his time to make sure I was all right. It saddened me to think that I would not do the same for him in America.

We waited for thirty minutes in front of the bus station. Bahia was nowhere. I called her and she said she was at the bus station. My escort took the phone and in Arabic found out that she was at the end of the bus line, which they call the bus station but I call a bus stop. Then we trudged up a long, steep hill to where Bahia was standing with a friend who teaches in a village. As an aside, this friend, Najah, told me that she was lucky to get the teaching job in this tiny village but she has a two-and-a-half hour commute each way. I made her repeat this three times before we agreed that she had a five-hour daily commute. This reconfirmed my feeling about the depression and hopelessness of the Moroccan student and I realized that Bahia, no matter how smart she was, had little hope of satisfactory employment.

About thirty minutes later we arrived at the apartment of Drissa, her parents, and eight single brothers and sisters. She lived in a three-story apartment building. There was a man in a sport shirt and pants sitting on a low stool at a low table butchering a cow on the landing outside of her apartment. The carcass of the cow was cut up into about six large pieces that were sitting on one edge of the table. There was a big washtub on the floor and each cut piece of beef was tossed into the tub. Even though it was warm, there was no refrigeration or attempt to keep the meat in a sanitary way. The once live cow was a gift from the groom who had it earmarked as the meal to be served at the wedding feast.

Her mother and sister greeted me warmly. The bride, Fatima, was propped up at the end of the long salon with her elevated hands and feet on white satin pillows letting the henna dry. Fatima was wearing white satin pajamas which she had donned after having come from the *hammam* (public baths). She looked exhausted. The nineteen-year-old bride was marrying her first cousin from Holland whom she had known one year. She met him briefly for the first time a year ago and the rest of the courtship has been through letters.

"Fatima has never been anywhere outside of Tetouan or Tanger," Drissa whispered. "She's worried. She's scared about moving away!"

I nodded sympathetically and was worried too.

Everyone there was a sister, cousin, or aunt except for Bahia, Najal, and me. The henna lady had a line of people waiting to get their hands done but they pushed me into line first as the honored guest. Everyone kissed me while mumbling something in Arabic. I gave my practiced idiotic smile and said nothing. Their ninety-two-year-old grandmother, with eyes closed, was singing to the prophet Mohammed, while everyone was sitting on the long narrow couches that typically line the walls in all Moroccan salons.

The mother brought a teapot of delicious mint tea and five glasses, one of which she filled for me first. She offered me a cookie, but I refused with a smile, nod, and *"La, la, shokrun."* She gave it to me anyway. All of the women wore scarves even though there were no men present. Najal wore a black scarf and I asked her to take it off so that I could see what she looked like. She was so breathtakingly beautiful that I gasped when I saw her. It dismayed the American in me to see these beautiful young women make themselves so unattractive, shrouded in shapeless *jallabahs* and plain scarves that tend to make them look like nuns. I asked to see Drissa's hair. She took off her black scarf, put her head down to her waist, shook her hair and looked up. Her hair was wavy and neutral like the rest of her.

She said, "Gloria, I can't wait to take my scarf off so the man I marry will be dazzled."

"When will you do that?"

"The day before my wedding." Her eyes glistened as she imagined the scene.

There was a little belly dancing, lots of joking, grandchildren running around, and chatter. The women were very nice, hefty, and unadorned. Most could speak no English. I spoke to one aunt in present tense Spanish. I am having so much fun with the Spanish I am learning at Cervantes Instituto. It amazes me that I even try to speak, but not being more fluent is a handicap. It takes so much strength to try to make conversations without much language. I was proud of myself that I was able to try to converse in spite of living in stereophonic babble for over six months.

I sat down on the couch next to Bahia. She leaned close to me and like Drissa, asked, "What religion are you Gloria?"

"Je suis croyante."

"I'll help you find Allah so we can pray together."

"Sweetheart, I am happy with my God."

"But Paradise is only for Muslims."

"Oh Bahia, I hope there is a little place for me there even though I'm not Muslim. Remember, I, too, believe in the one God."

She looked at me with her exquisite shiny black eyes. "Gloria, I know that you'll be there because I love you so much. And, the most wonderful part about Paradise is that everyone will be speaking Arabic."

"Bahia, that's the best thing you could've told me because I was the dumbest one at the Arabic school. I spent three miserable weeks trying to get beyond the alphabet."

"Your Arabic will be perfect!"

"Will I have a Moroccan accent?"

"Absolutely," she giggled.

She hugged me. I turned to leave and thought that it would be wonderful if I could ever tell these hospitable people about myself. I wanted them to understand my soul. However, I knew that could only happen in Paradise.

AND NOW WE ARE TWO

Ismael and Elizabeth insisted on taking me to the airport to pick up Dick when he arrived in November. He joined me on November 8th and planned to stay for seven months. I had intended to hire a taxi for the round trip but when Ismael learned that, he insisted on picking me up after collecting Elizabeth from work. I probably could have run to the airport I was so excited, but the Benbouhia coach was ready and waiting.

We watched the small airplane from Casablanca reflect the blinding sunlight and land at the Tanger airport. I felt like a sixteen-year-old girl. Dick got off the airplane holding two newspapers in separate rolls, wearing Levis, a long trench coat, umbrella, belly pack, carry-on Eiffel Rollaboard, and running shoes. I again realized that we, the sojourners, really do look different. I hadn't seen another American in weeks and it was a shock. Most certainly, we did not look Moroccan.

The four of us started giggling and all talking at the same time. It was obvious that this group was a foursome that clicked from the beginning. I felt so good at having my husband here and also seeing that he and my best friends had instant rapport. I had worked so hard to adjust and integrate. Now I felt like I was enjoying dessert.

They dropped us off at the apartment where Dick said, "I want to lie down for just thirty minutes. I've been en route for twenty hours."

"No! You'll sleep all day and be up all night."

Suddenly there was a power shift in our relationship because Dick was now in my territory and he had to fit into this world that I was a part of. He agreed to go walking and we entered Tanger together that sunny afternoon in November.

We walked outside our building where both day guards came over to meet Dick. I introduced him and told him to touch his heart after he shook their hands. They laughed because he showed them he was a Moroccan whose happiness at meeting them came from his heart.

The day guards at our buildings earned one hundred dollars a month. Mustafa prayed many times a day on a grass mat in a cubbyhole near the front door. Every time I saw him pray, head touching the top of the prayer rug, barefoot soles looking up to Allah, I couldn't help staring at his smooth, meaty feet because his toes were like little round cherries attached to soles that had no lines or calluses. I hung around numerous times trying to see what the tops of his feet looked like, but I was never successful. It was almost like meeting someone who had no fingerprints. Mohammed, the other day-guard, must have prayed inside because I never saw him on his prayer rug. However, they both had beards, which symbolized their piety and dedication to Islam and Allah.

The night-guard, whom Dick met later, earned one hundred and fifty dollars a month and seven nights a week he perched on an abandoned automobile seat stationed against a wall near the three buildings. He sat in that chair all night, while next to him were three wild dogs tied with ropes. The dogs growled constantly and strained at their tethers whenever anyone walked by. Abdelatif fed the dogs raw chicken legs. He would throw the legs onto the concrete steps and that was their only meal. The butcher gave me bones whenever I went to Sophia Grocery Store and I always threw them to the dogs as a peace offering. Now they sang when they saw me instead of their usual roar. I was scared to death of these dogs but felt that I may have ingratiated myself with them with the gift of bones.

About 6:30 every morning, there was a "changing of the guard." The day-guards went on duty and the night dogs were locked in the bowels of one of the buildings. Abdelatif would then mount his ancient bicycle to ride home with the tails of his colorful robe flying in the breeze. Mustafa and Mohammed assumed their posts, waiting for their day to begin.

About this time, Boutainia, the building maid, walked up to her husband to say she had finished her work. The wife of the day-guard Mustafa, she washed the steps three days a week, all ten floors, three buildings, on her hands and knees, using heavily chlorinated water. Boutania never smiled and looked chronically exhausted. Some days I would find her standing next to her buckets of water looking into space. What could she be thinking? Whatever it was, it was laden with fatigue. Today she looked like she could barely walk, but now her day here was over. She did not look Dick directly in the eye but, instead, looked down at her swollen feet barely covered in black leather sandals.

I grabbed Dick's hand and we walked to the street. It was only after we reached the street, hand in hand, that I realized that it was not a wise thing to do. Public display of affection between a man and woman was frowned upon, and after having my husband here for one hour, I had already made a *faux pas*. I had so much to share with Dick and wanted him to be part of this world that had been so difficult for me to enter.

The first place we walked to was the grocery store. Here was the "shrine" I visited at least once every day.

Sophia supermarket was perhaps the size of a two-car garage that has two long aisles. At the rear of the store where the curve of the inverted U comes is a cheese and meat counter. The owner imported delicious European cheeses. Ismael told me that most of his stock was mysteriously acquired because imports were really difficult to get through customs. I never knew how, but if I wanted something, I drew a picture or wrote the brand name on a card. I told Dick he could order anything he wanted. For his first request, he wrote *Kellogg's Rice Krispies* and the next time we were in the store, there were boxes of *Kellogg's Rice Krispies* waiting to go home with us. This little store stocked everything and, if you didn't see it, every five feet there was a boy in a long gray cotton coat who would find it for you. It was here that I had bought a whistling tea-pot, M & M's, deodorant, bittersweet chocolate, Danon yogurt, diet cheese slices, diet Coke, skim milk, Spanish olive oil, French baguette, Del Monte tomato sauce, Earl Grey Breakfast Tea, Cadbury's chocolate, a soup pot, etc. There was nothing they couldn't find for me especially since accommodating and overcharging foreigners was an accepted and preferred mode of business.

The boys in the long gray coats were warm, attentive, and friendly, as they helped customers and watched for shoplifters. Two days before, I had seen a little gray-coated guy with a huge moustache and kinky hair outside, unmercifully clubbing a poorly dressed Moroccan man because he had stolen a banana. Poverty was everywhere but the owner of Sophia grocery would not let it enter his door. However, lines of beggars waited outside his doors, hands out, wretched mutilated limbs displayed, while they wailed in Arabic.

Across the street from Sophia was the Internet Café Club International, run by Mohammed and his wife, Drissa. He was a native of Yemen and she was from Fes. Mohammed told Dick, "We had a better chance to make some money in Tanger, so we moved away from our families, which is unusual for Moroccans but not for you Americans." Ordinarily, Moroccans choose to live near their families and have couscous every Friday.

Mohammed and his wife were college graduates who could not find employment. He didn't say where he found the money, but somehow he borrowed enough for six computers and opened an Internet café. He worked from ten in the morning until two or three in the morning or until the last person went home. Then he cleaned the café and the toilet that he rented from the building owner, which was disgusting even when clean. Mohammed, like most Moroccan men, was scrawny and dark. He had a single eyebrow that traversed his face from temple to temple. His beaked nose was constantly red because he had allergies. He was tall for a Moroccan, over six feet three inches, with a heavy beard and always looked unshaven. He charged eighty-five cents an hour to use a computer but if you bought a twenty-dollar card, it was merely sixty cents an hour.

He and Drissa were fluent in French, Spanish, and English in addition to their native colloquial and Classical Arabic. She had gone to Michigan State to study one summer so her English was excellent. They were true Moroccans because they were polyglots. I learned that Moroccans absorb language through their pores. So here Mohammed and Drissa worked at their own business on the mezzanine of an almost empty building.

Today, Mohammed had to leave but we sat down and began writing to our loved ones. This was Dick's first day but he was already addicted and was busy describing his entry into the Arab culture. Mohammed's assistant, Driss, stood by smiling and waiting for us to give him something to do. Driss was a deaf boy who did not go to school. I don't know how old he was but he had the beginning of a moustache and dark peach fuzz. He was about five feet four and weighed less than one hundred pounds. Mohammed employed him or allowed him to stay at the Internet café everyday because Driss would run to a café to get the customers a coffee or mint tea for a ten- or twenty-cent tip. He spoke with the tones of a deaf person. Sometimes, Driss watched the shop while Mohammed ran out for a sandwich or an errand. There were times that Driss and I were the only ones in the café when the phone would ring. We knew it was important because Moroccans don't call just to chat. However, there I was with Driss, who couldn't speak or hear, and me who only knew English. Neither of us could answer the phone. Sometimes the phone rang incessantly.

I always said to Driss, "What should we do?" but he couldn't answer me because he didn't know what I was saying. Today, the phone began ringing and Dick said, "Answer it."

"What language do you want me to speak?"

"What happened to your Arabic?" he asked.

"I can count to ten and say the alphabet."

"French?"

"Few people understand me," I admitted. "I can sing '*Puff, Le Dragon Magique*' in B flat.*"*

So we sat.

When Mohammed returned, we told him about the phone and he became upset. After that, when we were in the café listening to the phone ring, we neither answered it nor reported it to the owner, which seemed easier for everyone.

We asked Mohammed about Driss' deafness.

"There's a lot of deafness in Morocco... Tunisia too. Kids get terrible ear infections. They're poor. They can't afford a doctor or antibiotics. So the babies are deaf."

Outside the entrance to this large, almost empty building was Mohammed's friend's business. Another Mohammed, also a college graduate, had purchased a one-meter's width table made of rattan which was common equipment for street sellers. Here, this Mohammed sold cookies for ten cents a pack, Marlboro cigarettes where you could buy one cigarette at a time, candy by the piece, and gum. These sidewalk peddlers were on every corner and at the entrance to every bank, store, or public teleboutique. This was a cash business which was a way of making a few pennies each day without begging. Even though Sophia market sold the same cookies, Bimo Tonik, which I bought every day, I always purchased them from a street peddler just because it was such a hard life for them. They sat outside in the merciless sun, cold rain, and westerly winds without protection. They had large pieces of plastic that they covered the inventory with when it rained, but they stood there outside, sad, vulnerable, and unprotected. During tangerine season, many sold tangerines which grew profusely in Tanger and supposedly were developed here. Thus, they were named tangerine.

I introduced Dick to my cookie "dealer." I told him about all the different kinds of cookies that were packaged four to a pack unlike our Oreo or Pepperidge Farm brands. He bought one of each just to taste the various kinds and to deplete Mohammed's supply of cookies. Mohammed was thrilled with the sales, while we had a good time getting high on sugar. Every time I looked at Dick in this altered environment, I grinned and said to myself, "He's going to like it here. He's going to like it here."

We had a good daily and weekly routine with the grocery, the cyber café, a produce market, the bank, post office with the international newspaper stand, friends, Spanish classes, work and excursions. Dick lectured at our school and I smiled everyday.

Ismael had arranged for his brother, Adnane, to invite Dick and me over to his house on Fridays for couscous. So when the two brothers, wives, and their children met on Friday at noon for couscous, there we were, adopted, interloping, eating and loving the day. We were the only strangers ever at the Friday meal and while we knew they really wanted us, we always felt that we had no way of repaying them. This made me feel guilty. I was told that it was an honor to dine at the table of Adnane Benbouhia. It was an honor to dine with both Benbouhias, but Adnane was the rich one.

I dedicated my year to Ismael and Elizabeth because I don't know how I would have survived were it not for them. I love Ismael, Elizabeth and Aziz. They gave so much time to us. They invited us over every few days. They worried about us. They fed us. They nurtured us. They loved us. They instructed us. However, they will never know any more about me or who I really am because I could not tell them I was Jewish. I was a coward. I could not get through the year without them and the thought that they might abandon me was paralyzing to me. They asked. They asked a lot.

"What religion are you?"

"*Je suis croyante*." I am a believer.

They asked. "Where do you go to church?"

"Our church isn't here."

They asked, "How does your family celebrate Christmas in California?"

"So differently than you here. You'd never recognize it as the same holiday."

"How are you going to celebrate Christmas here?"

"We're going to Marrakech."

"What kind of a name is Marchick?"

"It's Polish or Czech or Slovak. We're not sure."

They asked, "What religion is your cute daughter-in-law Pam?"

"She looks Spanish, doesn't she?"

"What religion is Dick?"

"Same as I am."

"Your two children, David and Patti don't look alike."

"Patti looks like a typical Irish lass."

"Why do you shop at the Jew's store?"

No answer.

I wanted to share our heritage with him because of the similarities I saw everyday, but couldn't. When Elizabeth and Ismael laughed with us and looked at us with the love of siblings, I would shiver and imagine the look turning to revulsion if they knew I was Jewish.

ABUN

Out of all my students, I choose Abun to describe because he was not too different from any of the others and his home was one of the many student homes I was invited to for Friday couscous. Abun was tall, painfully skinny, big smile, thick eyebrows, pug nose and shiny tan skin peppered with pimples.

This particular Friday had been the end of a four-day nonstop rainstorm. Abun and I took a bus to a village called Larosse that was about two hours from Tetouan and one taxi ride away from Martil. When we arrived in Larosse we walked through puddles to get to the inter city Mercedes taxis and rode another half-hour to his village. I had no idea how big the village was or how many people lived there or even the name of it but we were there. An old friend from Abun's high school met us by chance and he too was invited to join the family for couscous.

The three of us set out walking ponderously in the wettest mud that I have ever slogged through. Every step was an effort because my shoes collected more and more sludge as did the boys' shoes. We arrived at an unpainted door on a muddy street and Abun said, "First, you meet my grandmother. Then we go to my house."

An old woman opened the door, kissed Abun, kissed me on both cheeks and ushered us into the front salon. Immediately, she turned on the TV. This had happened in other homes and I wondered whether it was the custom or perhaps a status symbol to have a TV as a major form of entertaining a guest. I removed my encrusted shoes and sat down on a couch. Then, two of Abun's aunts came in carrying their babies, followed by their two unshaven husbands and a toothless brother. Evidently, all the men in the family except Abun's father were unemployed and they lived with the grandmother. The women kissed me on both cheeks and I returned the kisses.

They conversed in Arabic for a while, Abun tilting his head towards his grandmother and smiling, while I smiled dumbly, trying to appear as if I understood the conversation. Then we left after we repeated the kissing ritual. His sixty-two-year-old grandmother walked us to the door and stood there until she could no longer see us.

After we resumed our mud parade, we crossed the railroad tracks to four new houses and made our way to the last house on the street. Abun proudly pointed to his new home. Our shoes were impossible to lift so we slipped out of them before we entered and were greeted by his mother who wore a pink *jallabah*, black scarf, and carried a lantern. We kissed. His tall, quite handsome father followed carrying their baby daughter. Again, I was the only one who did not speak Arabic while Abun and I were the only English speakers.

The ages of the children were Abun, 23, Mourad, 21, Fatima 18, and the baby was 2. He told me his mother and father were both forty-four and they had married at a young age. His father looked thirty-five and his mother, fifty-five. They were dark skinned and his mother, who had a beautiful smile, seemed to have gray hair under her scarf. She was illiterate as were a great percentage of women her age.

They proudly showed me their new four-room house that had neither electricity nor running water. However, they did have a twenty-seven inch TV displayed prominently in the salon. They had no idea when their house would be connected to the public utilities.

Couscous was the meal of the day and I sat between Abun and his friend. Every word said by anyone was repeated in another language because of they, who speak French and Arabic but not English, and of me, who can speak three words badly in four languages. There was one piece of meat on the huge couscous plate and, as typical, we all ate from the same dish using tablespoons and shaping our own dugout in front of us. His mother kept putting the three-inch piece of meat in my cavern. I explained that I was a vegetarian and repositioned the single piece of meat on the top of the mound. Moroccans had trouble understanding why anyone who could afford meat or had a chance to eat meat would refuse. I finally said, "I have an enzyme," which seemed to satisfy them and every Moroccan after that. The mother then divided the one piece of meat among the family and the friend, who received the largest portion.

In the middle of the meal, the father got up and moved about eight feet from us and brought out a prayer rug to begin his evening prayers. He removed his slippers, got on his knees, placed his forehead on the floor and prayed. When he finished, Abun said, "Gloria, excuse me but I must pray now," and he repeated the ritual as did Mourad. After their prayers, they returned to dinner and ate.

I tried to talk to everyone and discovered that Mourad was studying violin in town. I said "*Mezyan*" in Arabic, which I thought meant "excellent."

Then I asked him how many hours a day he practiced. He conferred with Abun who said, "He doesn't practice because he doesn't have a violin."

I was going to ask how he could major in violin without the instrument but I knew that I would never understand the response even if it were explained to me in English.

Dinner ended. I excused myself and said to Abun, "Will you walk me to the taxi stand, *min fadlek* (please)?"

He was visibly upset and said, "Gloria, we expect you to stay here tonight."

I knew that I could not sleep there. I did not want to sleep in a house that had no running water, no electricity, no heat and no privacy. I wanted to go home.

"Absolutely impossible. *Min fadlek*, I need to go home now."

"There aren't any more taxis."

"Then I am going to walk to Tanger because my husband is sick and I need to go home."

A quick conference with his parents, bobbing heads bending towards each other, glancing at me after every other sentence, took what seemed like hours. I adjusted my clothing and appeared to get ready. I walked into the front hall where I had left my shoes with three pounds of mud. They were spotless as if they had been rubbed and polished by some genie. It didn't matter. I was going home.

"My father says there's a bus in ten minutes that will take you to another village where you might be able to connect with another bus that might get you to Tanger by midnight, but he's not sure we can get there in time."

"Abun, I'm history." He looked at me like I was crazy because he didn't understand the slang and right at that moment, I didn't care.

"We'll have to run. Can you run?"

I was out the door moving my pudgy little legs as fast as they could go. Not only was there a deluge but it was pitch black outside because, of course, there were neither streetlights nor houselights. Abun's father carried the one lantern from his home which meant that his mother was in absolute darkness. Abun grabbed my backpack. The father was puffing. I had a stitch in my side. Mourad ran ahead, turned and gave me his hand so I wouldn't fall into an unseen hole. Soon we saw streetlights. When the father reached a streetlight, he leaned against the pole and I saw a halo of light on the ground. We continued running through the muck and I wished that I had not drunk so much tea because I was about to wet my pants. The bus stop was empty but nearby there were two shadows. Abun stopped to catch his breath. I was ready to vomit. Mourad was wheezing and I turned to see an arc of light swing back and forth, slowly move in the opposite direction. His exhausted father was returning home.

Abun said, "The bus is late." Mourad mumbled something to him in Arabic and I stopped dead in my track and prayed that I did not have a heart attack. I was sweating like a horse and was literally covered with mud that splashed up when I ran through puddles. The boys looked like wet clay statues. What I saw was a surreal tableau as if we were part of a moonscape.

We arrived at the bus stop as the bus inched toward the stop. Abun explained to one of the passengers that I did not speak Arabic. I assume he asked her to show me how to get back to Tanger. The woman peered at me as she listened while nodding her paisley covered head.

I kissed Abun on both of his acne-scarred cheeks. "Thank you. *Shokrun,* Abun."

"*Shokrun Allah wajeeb,* Gloria." He asked Allah to bless me. I crawled up the steps of the bus and got to the window, waved and threw a kiss.

The stranger woke me two hours later, which meant that now it was time to transfer to a bus to Tanger. I got off the bus and noticed a dry mud trail behind me. I smiled and turned to board the next bus.

JAMAL

Jamal is my Spanish tutor. I look at him and marvel at his physical beauty. He is about six feet tall, and with shoes, briefcase and two books, a doctors' scale would register one hundred and fifty pounds. He always wears many layers of clothing. Rather than wearing them for warmth, he probably thinks they give him some bulk. His body has the grace and speed of a gazelle. He has curly dark brown hair, creamy white skin, large brown eyes and long eye lashes that would be the envy of any young woman. There is a thin vein that runs along his temple to his right eye and sometimes I can actually see it pulsate. It hypnotizes me so I cannot hear him question me. He repeats whatever he has said and I see that he is a bit impatient. It must be so dull to deal with a sixty-two-year-old woman who speaks only in present tense regular verbs.

He was blessed with perfect teeth that he brushed four times a day because his mother had no teeth and Jamal was determined to keep his teeth for a while. He asked me if my teeth were real and was surprised that I had never lost a tooth. I gave him floss, Crest toothpaste and Listerine mouthwash with explicit instructions. Dick even showed him his teeth and told him that his teeth were sixty-six years old.

Never having had a job, Jamal celebrated his twenty-ninth birthday with no imminent employment. I was his first employer. At twenty-three, he graduated from my university, Abdel Malek Saadi, having majored in Spanish and something else that I never could figure out. His one word of English was, "Stop." I learned about him when I announced to my class in Tetouan that I was signed up for the second quarter of Spanish and had not taken the first. However, I was confident that my high school Spanish would come back after forty-two years! Ibraheem, a student in the freshman grammar class, set up my first meeting with Jamal. Jamal said he would take a bus from Tetouan for one-and-a-half hours each way and then walk to my house in Tanger from the bus station for less than five dollars an hour.

Ibraheem said, "Gloria, that's a lot of money to give a Moroccan. Besides, all he does is watch TV."

"Ibraheem, I can't pay him less than five dollars an hour."

"He doesn't expect more. He'll be happy with less."

"Tell Jamal I'll pay him five dollars an hour plus the bus fare both ways."

So after much negotiation, we settled on five dollars, plus bus fare.

Jamal was a devout Muslim who had never had a date. In Spanish, I asked him *¿Porqué?* He replied, *"No dinero,"* and also because he was not allowed to date until it was time to get married. His constant companion was the hopeless realization that he would never have a job because the statistics were clear—fifty percent of the college graduates were unemployed and of those college graduates who had jobs, most of them were underemployed. Jamal was able to tell me that all of his friends were unemployed and depressed. They spent their days watching TV.

He arrived punctually at my apartment in Tanger three mornings a week. The first thing he did was put down his briefcase and go to my large front windows that had the most magnificent view of Spain, Gibraltar, and the Mediterranean. He looked through the high-powered Leica binoculars, which we left on the table next to the window, and he'd survey Spain. For me it was a visual feast, but for Jamal it was an emotional funeral. Most mornings I stood next to him waiting for him to speak, but usually it was hard for him to speak in any language. I knew and he knew that Spain accepted no more Moroccan immigrants. They were overflowing. National Spanish sentiment tilted toward the hope that all the Moroccan immigrants would disappear.

Tailing him, we would walk to the dining room table and my heart would say, "Don't look at Spain, Jamal. You'll never get there," but my mouth said things like, "*Me gusta mucho el mar. Me gustan mucho los barcos. Me gusta mucha la playa.*" (I like the sea. I like boats. I like the beach). He would give a small nod. He had to listen to more staccato sentences like that and to my terrible accent that he corrected constantly. I should write him to tell him that I have been complimented on my accent in my Spanish class in America.

One of the exercises we did each day was that Jamal would record my personal list of survival vocabulary words for me and, with my Sony Walkman plugged in, I listened to and repeated the words on my way to and from work. One list had the word for toilet so when Jamal read, "*El servicio*" he stopped, giggled, put his head down and flushed red. I felt stupid for being so insensitive to his naïveté. It was embarrassing for him to say "toilet" in front of me. In fact, I realized when he had to use the toilet, he asked Dick, not me, where the bathroom was.

The last week of my stay, Jamal said in Spanish, "Gloria, I want to go to America with you. I'll be your servant."

In present tense Spanish I said, "*No tengo un boleto.* I have no ticket for you."

"I could go in your suitcase and I wouldn't need to eat for twenty-four hours because I'm used to not eating during the Ramadan fast."

Jamal's beautiful face had turned to stone and his grim mouth appeared to have no lips. I recalled the present tense conversations we had about depression, no girlfriend, and no need to use future tense because there was no future. His home would always be with his widowed mother and older sister. He

OUR LIFE

One consistent aspect of contentment was the apartment in Tanger. Each morning, I awoke and breathed in the beauty of my world. The view of the Mediterranean changed from day to day and from hour to hour. As the sun moved, so did the prism of light that determined which jewel color would sparkle at that time never to be seen again. Some days the sea was the clearest blue imaginable while some days it turned slate gray or green. No matter what color, it was balm for my soul.

Spain also changed its colors. Sometimes the sculpted mountains were clear and chiseled and sometimes the clouds shrouded them, refusing you any glimpse of them. Shades of black and gray were punctuated with dots of light. The traffic was also visible from our aerie and those lights moved with the time of night and needs of the people.

My view of Spain was that of an observer enjoying beauty but I knew that the view to Moroccans, like Jamal, was different. Each day there were "boat people" who would crowd into a fishing boat or a rubber zodiac and try to illegally enter Spain. Each day most of these people were met by officials who immediately sent them back to Morocco. Sad, dejected, hopeless, and humiliated, they returned with new plans forming for their next attempt. These people looked at Spain as Paradise, hope, employment, democracy, and tomorrow. In addition to the Moroccans, there were refugees from sub-Saharan Africa who also made the trip. Every week, an empty boat was found floating in the sea because the passengers had drowned, and a day or two later one or two swollen bodies would wash up onto shore.

America. He too wondered about the Jewish power over America and American banks. I explained that that was a myth although he didn't believe me. I tried to eliminate these constant thorns in my everyday life. However, it was impossible.

One Thursday morning, Dick stayed in Tanger and I left for work in Martil. En route to the bus station, I fell into a hole and had mud up to my knees. There was no time to return home to change clothes, so I went to school looking like a happy pig, and the first people I encountered there were the maids.

From my first day at the university I had practiced my feeble Arabic with the maids. They laughed at my pronunciation and taught me one or two words each day. I wrote the words phonetically into my spiral book and actually built up a small vocabulary. One of my colleagues had seen me chatting with these young women, laughing with them, and waving goodbye to them, and she said, "Don't be too friendly with the lower class, Gloria. You'll be sorry." Of course, I smiled and ignored her advice.

On this muddy day, when I arrived on campus, the maids came up to me and started jabbering in Arabic. I motioned no and said, "*La, la.*" But they were not dissuaded from taking my book-bag and black purse and leading me by the hand to the room where they stowed their belongings. Each one of them grabbed a wet rag and started polishing me. They worked together and the result was that I was presentable by the time class began. I tried to tip them but they appeared to be insulted. I also needed to get some photocopies and did not have time to go to one of the Xerox offices, so they put an index finger in front of their lips as if to say, "Shhh." They had the key to the rector's office (the head of the university) and the secretaries' equipment. We sneaked into the inner sanctum and turned on the only Xerox machine probably in all of Martil that collated and had black ink. All the other machines printed

The final analysis was that I didn't know whether or not I had changed their minds about anything but I did try to give them honest and legitimate answers.

I slept all the way home on the bus and when I arrived I found that Dick had gotten the house ready for our first visitors, who were arriving by train the next Friday. We discussed buying a TV satellite dish for the roof and called Ismael to see if he would help us.

Early the next morning, Ismael and Elizabeth took us to an outdoor market called Tienda Barrata or Cheap Shop. Here we could buy everything and anything we wanted, most of which Ismael claimed was smuggled or stolen. There were several television dealers here who had competitive pricing. Items had price tags on them but no self-respecting Moroccan would pay the marked price. Ismael haggled with this media merchant for about ten minutes before they settled on a price for our TV dish. We paid cash. In addition, there was a man waiting there to install it for us. Again, Ismael haggled over the price. Dick and Ismael went in his car while the installer and I left in a taxi to return to the apartment.

The man, Abdelmoumen, carried all of the equipment plus the dish with him when we left and we all met back at home. Abdelmoumen told me in French, which I verified later, that he was a graduate engineer but was unable to get a job in engineering, so he hung around Tienda Barrata hoping for installation jobs. He felt very lucky to have managed generating this income. He climbed onto the roof of the building, dangled from the side of the roof, ten stories above ground, strung the cable, stapled wires, spent two hours installing the dish and meekly asked for the twenty dollars he had agreed upon. Ismael was a bit annoyed that he had agreed on that exorbitant price but it was getting late and he felt we might have to wait until tomorrow if he had really given him a hard sell! However, when Dick went to pay him, his money

handkerchief was hanging out of his pants but his wallet was safe. We tried to explain that they were poor and they were clever enough to know that we were going to have more money than the average Moroccan did. This didn't make anyone but Dick and me feel good because we felt like veterans.

We walked back after a wonderful day of poking around different stores and visiting the American Legation in Tanger. A tall skinny man with a bushy moustache sidled up to Dick and held a newspaper in front of him. I was walking in back of Dick and witnessed this incident. I yelled and when the man turned around, I realized that I had seen him approach Dick a couple of times before in the Medina. I screamed. Dick wrested the hand from his pocket and the would-be pickpocket yelled, "Jew! Jew!" We all stood there feeling guilty for some unknown reason. It was a draining experience.

When we returned to the apartment, the water was flowing a little harder so we stopped at the building president's flat and reported this. He wasn't interested but he thanked us anyhow.

After two days, the water flow increased, as did the smell.

Dick said, "That smells like toilet water."

I replied, "You're crazy."

Dave piped in, "Mom, it's a sewer."

"You sound like your father!"

By the fourth day, it was obvious that we were sloshing through urine. The liquid finally invaded the elevator and paralyzed it. Still, there were no repairmen. All the residents were now walking the steps as I did everyday. I had become strong while they were just beginning their training. Each day, we met new neighbors catching their breath as they rested on a landing during the ascent to their apartments. By the sixth day, it smelled like feces and there was no other way up the stairs but to wade through the effluvia. Finally after ten days, the elevator and the pipe were fixed but the smell remained.

The pictures were not the same. There were anti-American and anti-Israeli protest marches all over the Arab world including Morocco. We remained mute observers. Yet we stayed and were quiet.

Dick pressed send on the computer and the message was gone. The next day we received Patti's response.

Dad,
I already spoke to her about it. Her brownie leader called me because Rachel had shared with her troop that she has to pretend she is Catholic and celebrate Christmas in Morocco or else they will kill her grandparents. So I think she [got] the point. I am starting to really wonder about making this trip at all. I don't really know if it is a good idea for you to be there.
Patti

When Patti and Rachel came, it was the coldest, wettest two weeks in ten years. The rain was incessant. In fact, the railroad station closed because the tracks were submerged and no repairmen could fix them. Streets were flooded and the area surrounding our complex returned to its marsh status. We were living in a ten-story ark. One day, the water was so high that cars could not leave our subterranean garage. We had no car so we walked everywhere we could, but during these two weeks we walked in water. It was as if a sheet of slimy mud covered our whole city.

One day in the Medina, we noticed the pickpocket who loved Dick. I alerted Patti, Dick, and Rachel and we started working our way out. However, our "friend" had enlisted two of his colleagues and we noticed that they were starting to encircle us. We could not find a policeman so we started running to the edge of the Medina. The group started running after us yelling, "Jew! Jew! *Shalom!*" After this episode, Patti decided that she would rather shop at a mall even though they were nonexistent in Morocco.

THANKSGIVING

November 23, 2000

Thursday, Thanksgiving Day

Dear Family and Friends;

It is 6:30 A.M. on Thanksgiving Day, 2000, Tanger, Morocco. I am sitting in my living room looking at the lights of the Port of Tanger and waiting until it is light enough for me to feel comfortable walking the one-mile trek to the inter-city bus station. If I were in America, I would be getting up early in the morning, throwing on a pair of sweats, going for a five-mile walk around the reservoir and then would look for a coffee shop that was open in order to get my non-fat decaf *au lait*. And afterward, I would begin my preparations for Thanksgiving, whether it be just one dish for a potluck or many to host the dinner in my home. But this is not America and here it is not Thanksgiving.

An Intifada is being waged in this part of the world, and our quiet campus is now awakened with a purpose for which to live. The dull nightly newscasts that show one hour of the king's day suddenly has martial music broadcast with war pictures and, each day at 6 P.M., a song which is probably some Palestinian war song (I never found out) is played with pictures of dead Arabs from many wars. Non-involved colleagues who had never mentioned anything political to me now have something to talk to me about in the staff room and constantly ask my opinion about what is happening in 'Palestine.' Campus protest marches, student gatherings, and anti-Israeli rallies in the student meeting room accompany all of this.

The changes have affected both my outward and my inner life. For the past five weeks, students have been pulled

Rosh Hashanah had been the most memorable experience of my life. I can still see eight of us standing in a Moroccan Restaurant singing a *shehecheyanu*, lighting candles, eating honey, apples and pomegranates, and listening to the customers wish us a Good Shabbat and Happy New Year. We clung to each other and thanked God that we were able to celebrate as Jews in any country especially an Arab country. By *Kol Nidre*, I had been threatened in Arabic, abandoned by some of my dear American friends from the language school, and told to keep my identity a secret which I have done and will continue to do during my stay in Morocco. This is a heavy secret and one that makes me feel deceptive, phoney, and dirty. I walk with a cloud of sadness darkening even my happiest and most successful experiences.

My dearest friends here all have talked about the Jews. It hasn't just been how terrible they are, but it has been everywhere, whether it is saying, "See that shop. If you want to buy from a Jew, go in there," or on a tour of lovely homes, Abdelhai said, "That house is owned by a Jew." Ismael said, "If you don't like our wine, blame the Jews. They make it."

My good friend Latif said, "I love going to America but the universities have big problems. All of their departments of Middle Eastern studies have too many Jews. They ruin everything.?

When I told my dearest Fetouma that I bought something in a grocery store across from the Fes market, she commented, "But that's the Jew's store."

Elizabeth remarked, "I've got to get my car serviced at the Jew's garage."

We walk by the synagogue daily because it is on the main street but we do not even look at it because we don't want anyone to see our reaction. However, we cannot fail to notice the policeman and soldier always in attendance. Are they protecting the Jews or keeping the Moroccans away from the contamination? When I caught a pickpocket going into Dick's

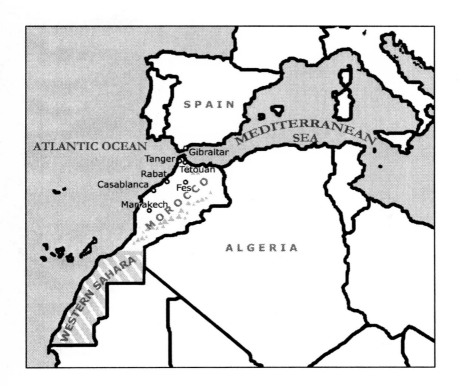

Everyone said I would be arrested.

 Every e-mail contained warnings that setting me loose in Morocco would be a disaster. My brother Bobby said the suicide bombers were going to use my body to deliver explosives. My brother Billy sent me twenty dollars to use as ransom. Dick told me to practice being timid. Even my dead mother warned me to be careful.

"Well, it always takes a long time because it has to go so far."

I motioned to Dick, rolled my eyes, and shut down my *Yahoo*. With a big smile, I said, *"Shokrun. Salaam."*

This sunny day was otherwise uneventful, so instead of beginning my forty-five minute walk to Spanish class at 5 P.M., I left an hour early in order to mail my granddaughter Rachel's journal to her. She had left it here along with train tickets, receipts, Bimo Tonik cookie wrappers, and maps of Morocco. Nameless memorabilia were arranged so that I could assemble it nicely in her book. This would be a pipe dream ordinarily for this uncreative soul, but here in Morocco I was capable of doing anything. Actually, it took several hours to paste this stuff in the book but I was determined to mail the creation to her today.

I thought I had already mastered the post office and that this errand would be routine. I even knew where to go without asking anyone. The customs office was located in the basement behind the post office and it was a cavernous concrete tunnel with an old wooden counter where two people waited for my business. This afternoon, it was not busy which was wonderful for my chronically impatient personality. I learned that you had to bring your unwrapped package to customs and then, after passing inspection, you had to wrap the package in front of the inspector and he would take it from you so that you could not put anything else into your parcel.

A bureaucrat in a blue suit was sitting behind the first counter. I walked up to him with a big smile and said first in Arabic, *"Saba al haire,"* and then continued in my pitiful French babbling, "I am a grandmother and my granddaughter Rachel visits her grandfather and me. She loves Morocco. I love Morocco and my husband loves Morocco." I droned on with my one paragraph of present tense French relating how much I loved Tanger and hated my house in Martil. The customs inspector didn't seem to be interested but I spoke

I yelled in English, "Now look what you have done to me. Stop! Give me my book *right now*." Of course, they did not understand anything I had said to them the whole time but my tone had changed. They stopped and there was silence in the entire place.

The first man opened the book to the map that I had gotten from the Moroccan Educational Council (Fulbright) or perhaps from Washington, D.C. and I looked at it. It was a lovely multi-colored map that displayed the different mountain ranges, valleys and cities of Morocco. Then they showed me the front of the book where I had pasted on another decal type map of Morocco but it was very small which is why I had added the large second map. Suddenly, a light bulb lit up in my head! I looked at the offending map and it listed the territory of the Western Sahara as a separate country and the cover map showed it all listed as one country. Western Sahara was annexed to Morocco in 1990. It was a bloodless but expensive addition. Ismael said that every working citizen had money taken out of his paycheck in order to pay for it. This was why every citizen not only believed in the political annexation but had literally "bought into" the addition. I had broken the law. I was guilty of not only civil disobedience but of inciting insurrection. I started shaking and leaned over to the centerfold and ripped the disputed map out of the book and the biggest of the three men grabbed the map out of my hand and confiscated the evidence. With that, my book was returned to me, and then I had to find someone to rewrap it and help me mail it. The room was now full and there were about twenty people who had crowded in to witness this scene, and to each I smiled as I walked quickly out the door. I thought I had seen it all and that there would be no more surprises, but I was wrong. The one decision I did make was that I was not going to mail any more packages to America.

fix her famous recipe. One morning, Salma and I spent three hours preparing couscous. She let me measure everything before she added it. I have since fixed the couscous twice and it was as good as Salma's.

I bought a couscous pot in the Medina because it was traditional and was a pot that you could make the meat in the bottom and then steam the grain in the top at the same time. However, in the United States, Chinese hardware stores have steamers or else you can make instant couscous with a mix and then cook the rest in a soup pot.

COUSCOUS

2 + lbs. Couscous from bulk section of the grocery. This is about 1 kilo
 ¼ cup water
 ¼ cup vegetable oil

Rub the oil and ¼ C of water into the grains of couscous and then let mixture sit in 3 cups of water for ½ hour so that the grains swell and will not fall through the holes of the steamer. Drain. Oil the sides of the steamer so that the grain will not stick. Add couscous. Put over boiling water for 1 hour. Remove and spread out onto a large tray. Add
 2 tablespoons salt
 2 ¼ cups water
Rub all the grains to remove the lumps. Add
 1 cup water Return to top of the pot and steam for about another hour. Taste.

VEGETABLES

These should not be overcooked and I tend to undercook them. Have the vegetables of your choice ready to be cooked in sauce # 1 but without the raisins.

White cabbage - blanched – about a half, cut in wedges (I use a whole head because I love cabbage & eat it the rest of the week. You can get by with ½ head white cabbage.

Acorn squash – Cut in slices.

Carrots   Cut in slices the same length as the squash or just throw in baby carrots.

Green beans Use blanched or frozen, throw in five minutes before serving.

Eggplant Slice it lengthwise

White and Sweet Potatoes Cut in wedges.

Red and green pepper Cut in strips.

Pumpkin Cut in wedges.

Turnips Cut in strips.

Zucchini Cut each in half.

Use any combination of the above vegetables according to your taste. Judge how long each takes to be cooked to your liking and line them up with the longest cooking ones closest to you. For example, I always put the carrots in first, about ½ hour before dinner. Then 5 minutes later, put in the pumpkin, peppers, turnips, eggplant, and potatoes. Last is always the cabbage and zucchini– only the last five minutes.

It is not necessary to use all the vegetables and you may decide to use only six fresh green beans just for the color.

A DECISION IS MADE

Each day we walked everywhere and, in spite of the routine, there was always something new that caught our interest and diverted us from our designated errand. Sometimes, when we passed a shop that had clean reflective glass in the front window, we would see an image that looked strange. Dick had on a baseball cap, Levi's, running shoes, a belly bag, sunglasses and a clean-shaven face. I would have dark glasses, lipstick, Levis, running shoes, a visor that protected my sun-sensitive eyes, a daypack and a sweatshirt. Compared to men and women in long robes, headscarves, skullcaps, a few with eyeglasses, beards or three-day facial hair growth and little makeup, we looked like aliens. However, the regulars knew we were not tourists and the beggars heard us say in French, "*J'habite ici*. I live here." In our neighborhood we were not targets of hustlers because we were recognized as residents with the exact reason remaining unknown.

Our integration into this world had been with some pain, some cultural abrasions and a lot of enthusiasm. The unsuspecting natives were doing exactly what they had been doing for thousands of years, minding their own business and I, a classical alien, was dropped into their midst. I was the odd one. I was the one who had to learn the rules and actually, I think I was a pretty good student in the end. However, there were *faux pas*.

On one of the days that I spent with my students, we had lunch in a casual outdoor counter café. After eating, I put lipstick on my dry lips. Bahia looked at me in horror. She said, "Gloria! Never do that again in public." It was a minor cultural abrasion but I had done it innocently. I never asked why it was so offensive but it may have to do with the more traditional

this with Ismael and within twenty-four hours, he made an appointment for me to see the best eye doctor in town who had trained in France and owned new French equipment. So, Ismael, Dick and I went to the doctor.

The exam was excellent and Ismael, our translator, our best friend, lovingly sat next to me while my eyes were dilated. The three of us chatted in English in the waiting room full of patients. I should say, Dick and Ismael chatted, while I planned my funeral. During the exam, Ismael translated my symptoms and the doctor listened, nodded, and looked. At the end, he said that my prescription had changed drastically in the five months since I had picked up new glasses and that was all that was wrong.

"Ismael, ask him if I have a cataract."

"I did. He said, 'No.'"

Dick said, "Ismael, tell him that Dr. Marchick thinks his wife has a cataract. And also ask him about her loss of peripheral vision."

The doctor listened and then straightened up as tall as he could stretch himself and said in Arabic, "I said Mrs. Marchick has no cataract. The loss of vision was temporary and it is nothing." Finally, he referred me to another doctor who concurred with his opinion. However, I still could not see. I still was uncomfortable in the sun. I still worried about my demise. I had my own kaleidoscopic view of the world through my diseased eyes.

Several of our American friends were ophthalmologists and I e-mailed them, in addition to e-mailing my own ophthalmologist. While they tried to reassure me, none could diagnose anything without seeing me and one said, "Gloria, you need to see a neuro-ophthmalogist."

The decision was made. I had to go home. I had to leave. I had to jump ship. I became so detached from the process at this time that, like a robot, I started making arrangements to return and separated my heart from my mind

One Thursday I was planted in the back seat of a packed taxi. There was a sudden cloudburst accompanied by thunder and lighting. This further compromised the limited visibility because the taxi had only one bad windshield wiper and no defogger. I was parked, stiffly upright, trying not to breathe nor add to the foggy windows when suddenly I heard a thump and I saw a sheep fly through the air only to land on the front side of the taxi. Mercifully, it did not crash through the cracked windshield into the front seat. I stifled a scream, turned around, removed my sunglasses, and saw that the sheep looked dead. The taxi stopped immediately and backed up a few feet to check on the sheep. He was dead. The driver and other passengers jumped out, leaving me alone in the taxi, and they started to drag the sheep over to the open trunk of the taxi. I was sure they were discussing recipes for lamb or mutton kabob. Suddenly, from nowhere, the shepherd appeared and he was hysterical probably because the sheep was dead, and he was even angrier that his sheep was going home with strangers. He yelled, waved a stick at everyone and they all quickly leapt back in the taxi, soaking wet while yelling back at the shepherd. The driver started the 'getaway car' and the shepherd began hitting the right rear fender with his herding stick. I cradled my green book-bag and black nylon purse in my arms and again was thankful that I was a vegetarian.

There is no day in Morocco without an incident and this day was no different.

My life was good here. My adjustment had allowed me to participate and observe this culture, this life and this adventure. I thought to myself that it was all right for me to leave. I needed to inform everyone that it was time to go.

Winning the Fulbright and then coming to Morocco was a dream. I knew it would be hard. I had eagerly anticipated the challenge. I chose Morocco because it had always been a country that existed in symbiosis with Jews in spite of being ninety-nine percent Moslem. Even today there are about five thousand practicing Jews here. Of course, I did not have the prescience to know that there would be an Intifada, nor did I know what the repercussions of it would be. I never would have believed that I would have been as uncomfortable as I was or as frightened. Being a closet Jew was not my intention. This was perhaps the greatest lesson of all and has been the hardest and most painful aspect of my stay here.

Yet, as I leave I realize that I have made marvelous friends, people who are truly sad to see me leave. My tutor is inconsolable. My Spanish classmates are sincerely sorry to lose the dumbest one in the class because now one of them will have the honor of that position! My university students are truly upset and have rallied around me like no other students ever would have. In fact, just last week I had lunch at the home of Ibraheem, a student whose blind father invited me to the school where he taught. I was treated like visiting royalty and with so much love. The next day I went to a wedding and henna party for the sister of another student. They sat me next to the bride and put henna on me only after the bride and before everyone else.

I feel that I am leaving a job not completed. This distresses me and obfuscates the great feelings of accomplishment that I was experiencing. Yet I know that with distance, this will all take on realistic proportions. The last aspect of my time here was the support I received through the e-mails people sent me. I was addicted to the cyber café and each day my transfusion of love, gossip, news, elections, etc. refueled me for whatever battle I had to fight the following day. I was reassured by each of you that I had a support team that was there for me and that on days when I felt like a real

"No Adnane. We won't let anyone do it. It's too early even for us to get up and I wouldn't let my own mother drive me. In fact, I'd like to not go myself."

"Then I'll send my driver Mustafa for you at five. He gets up early to pray."

"No, we have too much luggage and need a van. We've already paid for a car service." I was adamant.

Finally the Benbouhia boys gave up. We felt so cared for.

I have to decide what to leave and what to take. I am hoping I will be able to come back for finals in May so I have to leave books. If I do not come back, I will be unable to get anything, so tough decisions have to be made. I make another bag for Nijia, the maid, with my Moroccan umbrella, more dishes, more clothes, and more food that I had bought the day before to give to her. I have to put a note on it for my across-the-hall neighbor, Rachid, who will give it to her when she goes to work for him. I hope the bag is not too heavy since she walks over an hour to get to work.

I know Nijia will miss me. She is a forty-year-old illiterate who speaks Arabic and says she speaks Spanish. However, after I started taking Spanish once we got past *Señora*, which she called me, there was no conversation. She worked for me three days a week for twenty dollars. She scrubbed our two thousand square foot apartment on her hands and knees and dried it with a super-absorbent "drying towel." Barefoot, head covered and incessant, our shapeless human buffer cleaned and polished with dedication. Barely five feet tall, she moved every piece of furniture three times a week to clean under and around it.

Each day, I had bought a croissant and sweet roll for her. We asked her to have a cup of coffee at the dining room table with us, but she refused. Standing in the kitchen, at the counter alone, she ate breakfast. I dragged a stool and a folding chair next to the counter for her, yet she defiantly and deferentially stood. One day, without thinking, I closed the kitchen door and it was only then that she sat down and ate her breakfast, quietly, slowly, and alone.

Here bread is ten cents a loaf, so Dick and I never eat bread that is a day old. However, Nijia happily takes our *stale* bread home. Also, I fix extra food the night before she comes and send the "leftovers" home with her. She has neither running water nor electricity. There is no social security in Morocco, so she must work until she dies. My twenty dollars is

instructor has made some extra worksheets for me to do. I have tried to explain in Spanish that I am going to the *"estados unidos"* for a few weeks. The class is wonderful, as always, and the two hours fly. The students wish me *"Bueno suerte,"* and say in Spanish that they hope I will return soon. I assure them I will.

John has a big package in his backpack for me and he presents me with a beautiful leather hassock that is far more expensive and nicer than the one I bought for myself. It is beautiful, so again I cry. I give him a big kiss and notice the guard has stopped to watch the rare public display of affection between a man and a woman, especially a man and woman not married to each other. We laugh and converse in Spanish, me in present tense, John in present and past tense. Even if we knew it, we would not use the future tense. I learn that he quits the class after I leave Morocco.

When we leave the building, Ali, my regular taxi driver, is waiting. He is so sad that this is my last taxi ride with him. I give him the regular fare and an additional ten dollars, which I tell him is for taking his baby to the new McDonalds in town. It is too expensive for him otherwise and he is terribly touched by this gift.

He says, "I love you Gloria. I will never forget you. You are a Moroccan. I can tell by your heart. You think like we do."

We sit in the taxi for about twenty minutes talking about Morocco, his family, and how much he has loved being my friend. I want to tell him that I am Jewish. I start to but then I realize that it will achieve nothing. He will be unable to quiz me on how I feel about anything and will never learn anything about me. So, I get out, kiss Ali, and say, *"Bislammah and salaam,"* to my dear friend who smiles from ear to ear when he is in my presence.

As a hostess gift, I take a folding chair to Fetouma and a roll of heavy-duty tinfoil. Both of these items are treasures.

I continue, "Secondly, you would've had to leave your house at 4 A.M. to get us to the airport and neither your car nor any of Adnane's cars is big enough to accommodate our seven pieces. And, lastly, dear Ismael, I love you too much to bother you. I'd hate myself if I allowed you to ruin a day by getting up at 4:00 in the morning."

Nothing.

"Ismael, I hope you've heard me."

There was more silence. I waited. My throat tightened. My emotions were about to explode.

I waited and finally said, "Ismael, you will never in your whole life know how dearly I love you, Aziz and Elizabeth. To hurt you is a heinous act. Trust me when I say, I'm so sorry."

All Ismael said was "Good-bye," and hung up. I sat with the phone next to my ear and did not move. "Good-bye, my Ismael. Good-bye. God bless you."

Like Ismael, Fetouma wanted to drive us to the airport our last day in order to catch our plane at 6 A.M. but again we refused to allow it. She said that I hurt her feelings but the morning we left, a beautiful tan face yelled "Good-bye," to us from a crack in the door on the sixth floor of our building,

"Good-bye dear Fetouma. You have given me so much. *Bislammah and Salaam.*"

I finish packing at three in the morning and take a quick sitting shower on a pink plastic stool. I pour buckets of hot water over me. Instead of putting my pajamas on, I get dressed and lie on top of the covers to wait for 4:30 A.M. to arrive. I probably doze off but do not feel I have.

The night is dark. The dogs bark. Spain is lit up and there are some boats in the sea. I have looked often and long at Spain, Gibraltar, and my own personal sea. To this view, I silently say my last good-bye. I count the minutes and check my passport and my money every fifteen minutes. My apartment is spotless and barely looks inhabited. The wall of

EPILOGUE

I returned to America with a sad heart because of my unfinished year in Morocco. My e-mail was filled daily with letters from my students. Each one begged me to tell them the date I was returning. By the time I finished going to different eye doctors, it was too late to return because classes ended in March. I realized that I would never see my students again. They were relieved to hear that I had the beginning of cataracts in both eyes and that the loss of vision was an ophthalmic migraine. I was sad to hear that almost all of my students flunked the finals for my courses and would have to repeat the year. I was angry but decided that it was their system and while it shocked me, it probably didn't shock them.

On September 11, 2001, I joined every American watching the televised news. The fires, noise and even televised smells made watching unbearable, yet I was transfixed as an involuntary witness of the end of American innocence. I was thankful that I was in America where I would be comforted by others who were paralyzed by the same sorrow and horror as I was. I knew if I had been in Morocco, I would have come home on the first airplane. But I wasn't in Morocco. I was back in my own home and in a milieu that had some semblance of safety.

Friends from around the world called and e-mailed supportive, loving letters sharing the pain we were experiencing. The Benbouhias must have gone to the cyber café as soon as they heard. My dear pupils wrote expressing loving feelings and sadness.

Abun also wrote a lovely note that turned into a shocking ending. He was the straw that prompted me into immediate action.

September 16, 2001

Abun, my dear student,

I received your e-mail telling me how you worried about my country and me. I so appreciated the time it took to write and the love that I read in your letter. We had a wonderful few months at the university studying US History and going on excursions with Brahim, Bahia, Drissa and the other students from your class. I will never forget those times.

Historical events happened while I was in your country and I witnessed yet another Intifada in the land the Palestinians and Israelis both claim as their own. I watched Arab TV and then CNN and the BBC. The coverage of these events was different and here was my problem—I had to resolve what the "truth." was

I hope you comprehend the information in this letter because it is an important letter for me to write. I think it began when I applied for the Fulbright Lectureship that sent me to Morocco. I was so honored to receive this and then people asked why I had chosen Morocco. In case you don't recall this specific lecture, let me repeat that during World War II, the only three heads of state in the world to stand up to Hitler were King Carol of Denmark, King Bruno of Bulgaria, and King Mohammed V of Morocco. Hitler and the Vichy government demanded that the Moroccan Jews be delivered to him and your king defiantly replied, "I have no Jews. I have only Moroccan citizens." What amazing courage.

Because of this, I, a Jew, decided to go to Morocco to teach and learn about this fascinating Islamic country that had allowed Jews to live and thrive during these terrible times. However, I did not have the prescience (foresight) to know that there would be an Intifada. I had no intention of hiding my Jewishness. The first four weeks I was in Morocco, I lived in Fes, went to the synagogue, and celebrated the Jewish New Year with the students and staff at the Arabic Language School.

allows all of us, no matter how different we are, to live together and all of us to feel like Americans.

I hope you understand that this letter is to help you see me as I really am and know that no matter what, I treasure your friendship and the love you and your family showed me when I was a guest in your country. Even though I came to you as a teacher, it was I who was the student.

Thank you for sharing your country, your life and your family with me.

Salaam and Shalom.

Fondly, Gloria

The letter was written and I had "come out." Yet I felt no great relief. It was just another e-mail. Maybe I felt confident that Ismael and my other friends would never hear from Abun because professors and students don't mix as I did. They barely exchange greetings outside of class. In subsequent e-mails Abun responded with a new line. He now loved Jews and the "Hebro" people. Every letter was signed with *Salaam* and *Shalom*. I would never again hear how he truly felt and this was all right.

My normal life has resumed. I am going to New York City next week and to the platform to view what was the World Trade Center. I will thank God that I am an American. I will thank my God for giving me faith and a code of ethics by which I structure my life. I will turn and return to my ordinary existence. I will delete unanswered e-mail requests for my signature on Moroccan petitions that demand Ariel Sharon be tried as a war criminal. I will just be me. I guess that isn't so bad.

Gloria Becker Marchick has taught English as a Second Language (ESL) at Acalanes Adult School, University of California, Berkeley and Diablo Valley College for over twenty years. She has taught at the University of California, Berkeley, in the ESL teacher-training program and has taught at universities in the Slovak Republic and Morocco. She has won three Fulbright Fellowships. She lives in northern California with her husband. They have three children and three delicious grandchildren.